Safari Living
recipes

Published in 2003 by
Gallery Publications
P.O. Box 3181, Zanzibar
email: gallery@swahilicoast.com

London office:
32 Deanscroft Avenue
London NW9 8EN
email: zjafferji@aol.com

© 2003 Gallery Publications
Photographs © Javed Jafferji
Written and edited by Gemma Pitcher
Graphic Designer: Antony Chunguli
Designed by Zanzibar Gallery Publishers

ISBN 9987 667 23 6

Dedicated to my wife Kulsum Jafferji.

Other books in this series:
Zanzibar Style:
Voted one of the 'Top 20 travel books for Christmas 2001' by the UK's Times newspaper.
Zanzibar Style Recipes:
Recipes from Zanzibar's top hotels and restaurants
Safari Living:
Showcases Tanzania's top safari lodges and camps.

Front cover picture: Lake Manyara Tree Lodge, Tanzania.

Safari Living
recipes

Photographs by Javed Jafferji
Edited by Gemma Pitcher
Styling by Kulsum Jafferji

Gallery Publications

Contents

Introduction

'An army marches on its stomach'. This saying could also hold true for a safari. Since the times of the earliest pioneers, food and cooking have been an integral part of the safari experience. Nineteenth century explorers, such as Livingstone or Burton, had sometimes to exist on termites and grubs as they forged their way into the unknown. One menu prepared for early safari pioneer Vivienne de Watteville read:

Starter: Consommé (giraffe)

Second course: Tongue (of giraffe)

Main course: Tail (giraffe)

Which part of the aforementioned giraffe provided the dessert was unfortunately not recorded! Another traveller, Donaldson Smith, was happy to find fish on his safari table one night - until he discovered it had been cooked in Vaseline! US President Theodoore Roosevelt, it was reported, waited hungrily at the end of a hard day on safari for his meal of elephant trunk soup, oryx tongue and ostrich liver, followed by slices of elephant heart roasted on sticks over an open fire.

But ever since the continent became the playground of Europe's rich and famous in the early twentieth century, food standards on safari have been becoming ever more lavish. The white hunters of the 1930s and 40s considered it shockingly lax to entertain their film-star and industrialist clients with anything less than ten courses at dinner, all conjured from supplies carried laboriously on the heads of porters, or gleaned from game shot along the way.

These days safari cuisine has become more influenced by the flavours of the continent itself. African food is bold and colourful, with rich, earthy textures and strong, spicy undertones. Arab merchants, European colonists and Malay slaves have all influenced Africa's native cooking, resulting in a cuisine diverse and yet simple to prepare. But whether fly-camping in the bush or staying in a lodge, the day still begins with the traditional 'Full English' - bacon, sausages, tomato and fried eggs, more often than not cooked in a heavy iron skillet over a wood fire before dawn by the camp cooks. Fresh tropical fruits from the lowlands and hardy vegetables from cool highlands are always available.

Technology may have moved on somewhat since the days of the early safari pioneers, but today's bush chefs are nevertheless required to work miracles with the most basic of equipment and ingredients. The most essential element in safari cooking is the fire - at least six feet across, with ashes, flames and coals of varying temperatures for every type of dish. Fresh-baked bread is prepared in an old tin trunk over smouldering ashes, legs of succulent lamb are roasted by being buried in the earth in a nest of hot coals, or vegetable kebabs skewered on pieces of wood plucked from a nearby tree. Food is kept cold in gas fridges, packed in ice or simply brought into camp 'on the hoof'!

Ngorongoro Conservation Area

Biologically the southern part of the Serengeti ecosystem, the landscape around the world-famous Ngorongoro Crater is actually a sharp contrast to the waving short-grass plains of that lie to the north. Green, dripping rainforests are the predominant feature here, clinging to soaring, mist-topped highlands. The crater itself is breathtaking – the largest unbroken volcanic caldera in the world, home to a dazzling variety of big game, uniquely acclimatised to vehicles. In spring, a carpet of yellow flowers coats the crater floor, and bull elephants wade in knee-deep to graze, their white tusks in sharp contrast to the dark-blue hills behind them.

The Ngorongoro Crater Conservation Area is a ground-breaking experiment in multiple and fair land use, where pastoralism, conservation and tourism strive to exist hand in hand and in harmony for the greater good of the environment. As a World Heritage Site and an International Biosphere Reserve, the crater area is a showcase for Tanzania's conservation policy and an important learning ground for environmentalists the world over. But lest all this sounds rather worthy and dull, the magnificent, extravagant luxury of the Ngorongoro Crater Lodge awaits the visitor – gastronomic delights just as high on its list of attractions as outrageous décor!

Gibbs Farm

A stay at Gibb's Farm, a former working coffee plantation house in the fertile hills close to the village of Karatu, is a memorable culinary experience. The old colonial farmhouse, built by German settlers in the early 20th century, still has the character of a well-looked-after private house, with roaring fires and friendly service.

Fresh, organic ingredients are used to make a series of home-cooked, wholesome meals, served in a pretty dining room in the old farmhouse. The vegetable and flower gardens now cover several acres and everything is grown organically using only natural fertiliser from the farm. Plants with insect repellent properties are used instead of pesticides to ensure that no chemicals are added to the vegetables. The farm's cows and pigs provide some of the best meat available in Tanzania, and the chickens range freely to provide eggs of natural quality and taste.

Lunch is served buffet style and includes a wide selection of savoury pies, vegetable dishes, hot dishes, and salads, as well as a few traditional African dishes, followed by a tempting dessert buffet. Dinner at Gibbs is a lavish four course affair, accompanied by homemade bread and rolls and followed by tea or Gibbs' own coffee.

Tree tomato chutney

400g chopped tree tomatoes

400g onions, sliced

400g unripe papaya, peeled and diced

750g sugar

1 pint white vinegar

1 tsp salt

1 tsp chili powder

1 tsp ground nutmeg

1 tsp ground cloves

1 tsp ground cinnamon

In a large pot, simmer all ingredients for 1 1/2 hours until the fruit is cooked and tender. Store in sterilised jars.

Chicken and pasta salad

Serves 4-6

225g cooked macaroni, cold

1 roast chicken, shredded

2 green peppers, grilled and cut in Julienne

2 mangos, peeled and sliced Julienne

2 tomatoes, cut in julienne without seeds

75g diced cashew nuts

2 tbs tomato ketchup

200ml mayonnaise

Salt and pepper, and tabasco to taste.

Combine all ingredients together and serve.

Arugula soup

Serves 4-6

300g arugula leaves

50g unsalted butter

1 medium leek, sliced

1kg potatoes, peeled

2 litres chicken stock

Salt & pepper

Sauté the leeks in butter for 2 minutes but do not brown. Add the potatoes and chicken stock and cook for 30 minutes until the potatoes are tender. Combine arugula with the stock and vegetables, cook for an additional 5 minutes, then purée in a blender to desired consistency. Season with salt and pepper to taste.

Baked chocolate pudding

Serves 4-6

250g white flour

250g brown sugar

30g cocoa

200g melted butter

1 pint milk

3 tsp baking powder

Pinch salt

Mix all the ingredients together and pour into the greased baking dish. Mix 150g white sugar, 150g brown sugar, 30g cocoa, and add to the mixture. Pour in 2 cups of cold water and bake for 30 minutes at 350 degrees.

Pork and cabbage pie

Serves 4-6

Pastry:

300g flour

100g lard

1 tsp salt

120ml water

Filling:

1 tbs cooking oil

2 onions, sliced

225g minced pork

225g white cabbage, shredded

1 tsp nutmeg

Chopped parsley

Salt & pepper

Sauté onions for 2 minutes, add pork and cook for 10 minutes. Include the cabbage and cook for another 20 minutes until moisture has evaporated. To avoid browning, season with salt, pepper, nutmeg and parsley.

Pastry: Incorporate all ingredients and knead together to create soft dough. Line a 9 inch pan with a portion of the dough and save enough to form the top. After adding the filling, cover with the remaining dough and pinch bottom and top layers together to complete the shell of the pie. Bake at 350F until the pastry is sufficiently browned and flaky.

Ngorongoro Crater Lodge

Designed by top South African architect Sylvio Rech for its owners Conservation Corporation Africa, Ngorongoro Crater Lodge is one of Africa's most outstanding wildlife hotels. Perched on the rim of the Ngorongoro Crater, the Lodge is designed to resemble a traditional African village on the outside, with understated colours and patterns that fit into the surrounding landscape of dramatic hills and ravines. All rooms face towards the crater floor, visible through the mists like a huge patchwork quilt.

Inside, however, the subdued tone of the exterior vanishes abruptly, to be replaced with a bohemian fantasy of towering banana-leaf roofs, chandeliers, enormous art-deco sculptures and roaring fires. There's a fireplace in each bedroom, too, to protect against the cold highland nights, along with a couple of easy leather armchairs and a decanter of sherry. Dining is in the huge restaurant, reminiscent of an English stately home, with crisp white damask tablecloths, crystal glasses and silver cutlery.

For lunch, tables are spread with platters of cold meat, salad and cheese and moved to the panoramic outside terrace, with a spectacular view of the crater and the dome of blue sky above, where bateleur eagles float in the crisp, clean air.

Tunisian beef fillet

Serves 8

1 whole fillet of beef

1 handful coriander leaves

1 handful mint leaves

50g almonds

6-8 garlic cloves

Pinch of dried chilli

4-6 ounces of olive oil

120ml lemon juice

Salt and pepper

1 tsp special spice

Blend all ingredients except the oil. With the motor running slowly pour in the oil to make a paste. Pound the filet thin and spread the sauce over meat and marinate for at least 1 hour. Grill to medium rare only. Do not overcook or the dish will be bitter.

Prawn & coconut laksa

Serves 6

500g whole prawns, shell and head on

200ml olive oil

30g chopped lemongrass

60g tomato paste/puree

4 cloves garlic, chopped finely

1 cup grated fresh galangal

1 litre chicken, vegetables or fish stock

4 hot red chillies

200g sliced red onions

30g carrots, roughly chopped

The stalks from 1 bunch of fresh coriander

Salt & pepper

Cut the shell into 3 or 4 pieces, using all the prawn. In a large saucepan heat the oil until very hot. Add chopped prawns, and cook over a hot fire until well coloured. Add to this the carrots, onion, galangal & lemongrass. Fry for a further 10 minutes. Add tomato paste, chillies and garlic, cook for further 5 minutes. Cover with stock, bring to the boil and simmer for 30 minutes. Blend all in a liquidiser or food processor. Pass through a fine sieve 3 or 4 times. (This is to ensure that no parts of shell are left in the soup). Leave aside whilst you prepare the garnish.

Garnish for prawn & coconut laksa

50g short vermicelli pasta, blanched for 1 minute

200g shelled and de-veined prawns

30g red onion, quickly stir-fried

30g raw white of leek, thinly sliced

30g finely diced carrot, quickly stir-fried

1 tbs crushed garlic

1 tbs finely sliced ginger

1 green chilli per person

1 10cm length of bruised lemongrass leaf per person

200ml coconut milk

200ml freshly squeezed lemon juice

1 tbs fresh coriander leaves

1 tbs fresh mint leaves.

Dried red chilli flakes to sprinkle over the top.

Mix all the above together. Then add to the hot soup. Taste for seasoning, and if lacking small amounts of fish sauce may be added.

Apple crisp

Serves 6

100g all purpose flour

225g sugar

225g firmly packed brown sugar

150g quick cooking oats (breakfast oats)

1 tsp ground cinnamon

3 tsp chilled butter cut into small pieces

875g thinly sliced green apples

250ml thick yoghurt or sour cream

1 tsp cinnamon

3 tbs orange marmalade, warmed

Combine the first 5 ingredients in a bowl; stir well. Cut in butter with a pastry blender until mixture resembles coarse meal; set aside. Warm the marmalade to a thin consistency and toss with the apples. Combine the yoghurt with the cinnamon and apples. Place apple slices in a pre-cooked shell and sprinkle evenly with the

flour mixture. Bake at 375F for 35 minutes or until bubbly and golden. Serve warm, garnished with unsweetened whipped cream.

Chocolate chip cookies

Serves 6

125g butter

125g sugar

125g brown sugar

2 eggs, beaten

250g self-raising flour

1 tsp baking powder

1/2 tsp salt

175g dark chocolate chips

125g walnuts, finely chopped

1 teaspoon vanilla

Heat oven to 190C. Cream butter and sugars together. Add eggs and beat. Add sifted flour, baking powder, and salt. Mix to combine. Stir in chocolate and nuts and mix. Place spoonfuls onto a greased baking tray, allowing for room to grow. Bake 10 to 15 minutes until lightly golden. Cool and store in an airtight container.

Serengeti National Park

Giraffes moving across the sunset, acacia trees silhouetted against the dawn – the Serengeti has all the classic images of Africa wrapped up in 14,000 square kilometres of seemingly endless space, earth, and sky. Tanzania's most famous National Park is more popular than ever before, but hasn't lost its wild character, or the sense of freedom that accompanies a day spent driving through the southern short grass plains or around the kopjes of the west, perhaps hoping for a sighting of cheetah in the grass or lion under a tree.

Stopping is just as important as driving, however, for it is only when standing on a hilltop or sitting by a riverbank that the smaller details of the Serengeti come into focus – the buzz of insects in the grass, the distant boom of a hippo, the tiny, rustling movements of a nesting bird, or the creak of the wind in the treetops.

From the simple and rustic to the offbeat and modern, each of the Serengeti's luxury lodges and camps presents an entirely different face of the National Park. Their character and style – each distinct from the others – perfectly complement the unforgettable beauty of the park's landscape and wildlife.

Grumeti River Camp

A surprising and contemporary camp with funky modern décor based on vibrant colours and abstract patterns, Grumeti is perfectly placed to allow visitors an oasis of relaxation in the Serengeti's Western Corridor. It is here that the famous annual crossing of the Grumeti River by the migrating wildebeest and zebra occurs, an event that is as blood-curdling as it is exciting, with the river's enormous crocodiles snapping up the helpless herbivores as they plunge nose-deep through the water.

The river at Grumeti, however, is far more serene, a placid backwater covered with lily pads and filled with gently snorting hippo. Dining tables and chairs in bright colours, rendered in galvanised steel, are placed under trees by the water's edge for lunch. Chilled white wine, salad and home made ice cream are served on chunky, designer crockery as the fish eagles call from the trees overhanging the pool and the hippo, just yards away, sink up to their eyes among the green vegetation.

For dinner, classic Italian pizzas are regularly created in the camp's earthenware pizza ovens, accompanied by young green vegetables or crusty garlic bread. The dining room is an outside boma, enclosed by mud walls and lit by hurricane lamps, with the African stars dazzling overhead.

Ciabatta bread

Serves 4

For the starter

1 tsp dried yeast

150ml water

3 tbs tepid milk

1 tsp sugar

150g flour

For the dough

1 tsp dried yeast

250ml water

1 tbs olive oil

350g flour

1 1/2 tsp salt

Beef with marinated paw paw and green chilli

Serves 2

750g rump steak or sirloin steak or fillet

Cracked black pepper

Olive oil

4 tbs soy sauce

Lettuce, rocket and *mchicha* (spinach)

Green, red and yellow peppers thinly sliced

350g unripe papaya

2 green chillies shredded and chopped

Handful of fresh mint leaves chopped

Handful of coriander leaves

1 cup lime juice

2 large tbs fish sauce

2 tbs brown sugar

1 clove garlic, squeezed

Place the meat in marinade of lots of cracked pepper, soy sauce and olive oil. Finely shred the papaya and green chilli. Add the peppers. Combine it with the fish sauce, lemon juice and the sugar, mint and garlic. Grill the meat - must be very rare. To serve put mixed greens on a plate. Top with the meat and then the papaya salad on top. Sprinkle coriander over.

For the starter:

Sprinkle the yeast into a bowl and add the water and milk. Leave for 5 minutes and then add sugar. Mix in the flour to form a loose batter. Cover the bowl and leave to rise for at least 12 hours

To make the dough

Sprinkle the yeast into the water in a bowl. Leave for 5 minutes and then stir. Add the yeasted water and olive oil to the starter and mix well. Mix the flour and salt to form a sticky wet dough. Beat with a wooden spoon for 5 minutes. The dough will become stringy but will be too soft to knead. Cover with a towel and leave to rise until it has trebled in size - 3 hours. Do not knock the dough back. Flour two baking sheets.

Divide the dough in half and use well floured hands to pull and stretch the loaf to 12 inches long. Dust the loaf. Prove uncovered for 20 minutes. Bake for 30 minutes until risen and golden.

Chicken breasts with garlic and potatoes

Serves 6

3 tbs olive oil

8 potatoes peeled and roughly chopped

Handful fresh rosemary

20 cloves garlic

6 chicken breasts, skin removed

3 lemons, cut in half

Salt and black pepper

Toss the potatoes, garlic, olive oil and rosemary in a roasting pan and bake for 20 minutes in hot oven. Fry the chicken breasts on either side to brown. Place on top of roasting potatoes, cover and bake for another eight to ten minutes. Do not overcook. While this is happening place the lemons on or under a grill. This caramelises the lemon and makes it very juicy. Serve with a tomato and red onion salad tossed with balsamic vinegar.

Papaya and lime sorbet

Serves 2

150g castor sugar

425 ml water

1 lime, grated rind and juice

1 large papaya or paw paw

Dissolve the sugar slowly in the water then bring to the boil. Add the lime rind and simmer for 5 minutes. Cool completely. When cool, strain. Peel & chop the papaya, remove the seeds. Add the lime juice. Then blend until smooth. Combine with the syrup and spoon into the ice cream maker. Freeze churn until ready to serve. Serve in balls with a twist of lime on top

Klein's Camp

Klein's Camp, in the remote northern section of the Serengeti eco-system known as the Kuka Hills, is built on the site of a vegetable garden set up for other white hunters by Al Klein, one of Tanganyika's most colourful characters. Today the vegetable garden is owned and run by local people, who sell their fresh produce back to the camp's kitchens. Dinner is served in the stone and thatch bar, with a panoramic view of the surrounding countryside, which is given heat and warmth in the chilly dark evenings by an enormous wood fire in the centre, protected by an iron hood.

But in keeping with its historic past, Klein's is first and foremost an adventurous place, with guests spending far more time out in the bush than at the camp, convivial as it is. And where the guests go, the kitchen goes too – early morning game drives, for example, culminate in an enormous cooked breakfast, prepared by the safari guides on the latest state-of-the-art gas-fired barbeques. For dinner, a bush banquet is regularly set up in a clearing a few miles away from camp, hurricane lamps and a camp fire setting the scene for a lavish feast, cooked with panache on an outside stove.

Saffron chicken breasts with almonds

Serves 8

8 boneless chicken breasts

1 cup olive oil

200g red onions, finely chopped

100g crushed garlic

4 slices thick stale white bread, crusts removed

2 tsp ground coriander

2 tsp Spanish paprika

2 tsp tumeric

1 tsp crushed black peppercorns

100g almonds

100g chopped parsley

1 bottle dry white wine

500ml chicken stock

Salt

Rub the spices into the chicken breasts. Heat the olive oil in a large frying pan. Season with a little salt and fry quickly on both sides until lightly golden but raw on the inside. Remove from the pan and then gently fry the onion and garlic. Add the bread and allow it to soak up all the oil. Add the almonds and half the parsley. Pour over the white wine and bring to a simmer, then add stock. Season with salt and cook gently for 5 minutes. Return the chicken to the pan, lower heat to a very gently simmer. After 5 minutes turn breasts over. After a further 5 minutes the breasts should be cooked. Remove and keep warm as you reduce the sauce if necessary. Mix the chicken, sauce and remaining parsley together.

Pitta breads with black olives and cumin

Serves 6

6 tsp dried yeast

3 tsp sugar

840ml lukewarm water

3 tsp olive oil

135g bread flour

3 tsp salt

200g chopped black olives

100g toasted cumin seeds

Mix together the yeast, sugar, water and oil. Sieve together the salt and flour. When the liquid starts to ferment, start to add flour. Do this as you would a butter, slowly adding the flour giving it a good beating. Add the cumin seeds and olive pieces. After adding half the flour, you will have to knead in the flour with your hands. You should end up with a dough slightly looser than a conventional bread mix. Allow this to double in size, before knocking down. Cut dough into pieces weighing app. 100g. Roll into 1 cm thickness. Allow to double in size again. In the meantime, set the oven at 250c, or bush temperature very, very hot. Place in clean baking trays, so as to heat up. Sprinkle or gently brush breads with a little water and place on hot trays in oven. Cooking time is very quick. After only 45 minutes the breads should be well puffed up. Remove from the oven before they start to brown. If not using immediately, rub very lightly with olive oil and store in a sealed container

Tomato, chilli and coriander salsa

Serves 6

10 ripe tomatoes

2 red onions

3 red or green chillis

1 bunch coriander

Finely dice the tomatoes. Finely dice and fry the onions with 1 teaspoon of coriander powder. Finely dice the chillies. Roughly chop the coriander. Combine above with 1 tablespoon of olive oil. Then just before serving add salt, pepper and 1 tablespoon red wine vinegar.

Kirawira

irawira Luxury Tented Camp has gained a well-earned reputation as a place where the gentlemen (or lady!) explorers of the nineteenth century would not feel out of place. The camp is determinedly nostalgic in style, with a definite emphasis on the finer things in life. The walls at Kirawira may be made of canvas, but the interior spaces are furnished in grand style, with no concession to the camp's wild and remote location. Edwardian elegance is everywhere, from the straight-backed chairs of the sitting room to the fine blue-and-white china of the dining tent.

Bedroom tents look out across a stunning vista of dark-green plains, distant blue-green hills and wheeling birds of prey. Inside, pretty patchwork quilts and lace mosquito nets emphasise the vintage feel of the rooms, and vast bathrooms with black and white tiles and marble sinks are lit by old-fashioned brass lamps.

Dining at Kirawira is formal, with champagne for breakfast and five courses at dinner and lunch, all served by lamplight in the dining tent. After dinner, the softly-lit art deco private bar, decanters of port and sherry ready alongside the finest cigars, gleams temptingly, and leather upholstered armchairs beckon guests for a nightcap taken listening to the gentle sounds of the African night outside.

Tossed seafood spaghettini with white wine, cream and herbs

Serves 4

500g thin spaghetti

For the seafood sauce:

225g raw tiger prawns, shelled

225g cooked lobster meat

1 clove garlic, crushed

1 finely chopped onion

50ml dry white wine

2 tbs sherry vinegar

250ml fish stock

3 tbs double cream

2 tbs grated parmesan

1 tsp mustard

2 tsp tomato paste

Chopped parsley to garnish

Bring a large pan of salted water to the boil. Add the spaghetti and cook until *al dente*. Drain and set aside. Meanwhile, heat the oil and garlic in a large frying pan. Add the prawns and cook over a high heat for 3-4 minutes, or until the prawns have turned pink. Then remove the prawns from the pan and set aside. Add the chopped onion to the pan and cook for 2-3 minutes until softened. Then pour in the wine, vinegar and fish stock and, stirring frequently, bring to a boil. Stir in the cream, parmesan, mustard and tomato paste, and reduce until thickened. At the last minute add the cooked prawns and lobster meat to the pan. Cook for a further 2-3 minutes. In a bowl combine the spaghetti and the seafood sauce. Season with salt and pepper, and just before serving sprinkle over some chopped parsley and some parmesan shavings.

Rich chocolate orange mousse with chocolate leaves

Serves 6

170g plain chocolate

45g unsalted butter

2 tbs Grand Marnier or Cointreau

3 egg yolks

3 tbs water

3 tbs sugar

2 tbs orange rind

3 egg whites at room temperature

1/2 tsp cream of tartar

45g sugar

125ml cold whipping or double cream

Combine chocolate, butter and Grand Marnier in a large heatproof bowl. Set the bowl over a pan of simmering water and stir the mixture until the chocolate is melted. Then remove the bowl from the water and set aside. Whisk together egg yolks, water and sugar in another

bowl. Set this bowl over the pan of water and, whisking constantly, heat the mixture until thick and puffy. Remove from the water bath and fold into the melted chocolate, adding orange rind. Allow to cool to room temperature.

In a separate bowl, beat egg whites on medium speed until foamy. Then add cream of tartar and beat until soft peaks form. Gradually beat in sugar. Increase speed to high and beat until stiff peaks form. Using a large rubber spatula, stir one quarter of the egg whites into the chocolate mixture to lighten it. Then gently fold in the remaining whites. In another bowl, beat cream on medium/high speed until soft peaks form.

Gently but thoroughly fold the cream into the chocolate mixture. Turn into a 1.25l bowl or six 175 to 250ml bowls. Refrigerate for at least four hours before serving. To make the chocolate leaves, melt 50g plain chocolate. Select from your garden 12 appropriate leaves. Dip one side of the leaves in the melted chocolate. Arrange the leaves, chocolate-side up on a baking tray. Refrigerate, and, when the chocolate has set, tear away the leaves from the garden to leave the chocolate leaves.

Smoked sailfish cakes with lime vinaigrette

Serves 4

For the sailfish cakes:

8-10 slices of smoked sailfish

1 1/2 tbs fresh coriander, chopped

1 1/2 tbs fresh dill, chopped

1 onion, finely chopped

2 tbs capers, finely chopped

Seasoning to taste

Mayonnaise, for binding

For the lime vinaigrette:

4 tbs best quality olive oil

3 tbs lime juice

1 tbs cider vinegar

Seasoning to taste

First prepare the sailfish cakes. Combine all of the listed ingredients in a bowl, adding enough mayonnaise to lightly bind the mixture together. Then spoon the mixture into 4 medium sized pasty cutters that have been arranged onto a plate or tray. Place the tray in the fridge, and refrigerate for one hour before serving. Meanwhile prepare the lime vinaigrette by whisking all ingredients together in a bowl. To serve, place the sailfish cake in the centre of a large plate. Garnish as you desire, and drizzle vinaigrette.

Kusini Camp

Perfectly sited in a cluster of kopjes, the Serengeti's huge, granite outcrops, Kusini is a permanent tented camp blended seamlessly into the delicate environment of the predator-rich southern plains of the Serengeti. The surrounding short grass plains provide the setting for the most spectacular natural phenomenon in the continent of Africa, the wildebeest migration, during which time the hordes amass around the camp for the birthing of their young. But even during the dry season, the southern Serengeti is an excellent location for game, with cheetahs being particularly plentiful within just a few miles of the camp. Elephant are also almost always in close proximity, visiting the camp's waterhole daily in dry season and lurking at night among the trees that surround the tents.

Secluded amongst the rocky outcrops, Kusini's nine tents feature Edwardian style ensuite bathrooms with showers and elevated terraces overlooking the Serengeti plains. Between game drives, guests gather for candlelit meals and tall safari tales in the elegant dining tent, or have sundowner cocktails, early morning tea or even full banquet dinners on top of the huge kopje that dominates the camp, a steep scramble up the side being rewarded with a spectacular view of sunrise or sunset across the surrounding plains.

Florentines

Serves 6

90g butter or margarine

100g caster sugar

100g flaked almonds, roughly chopped

25g sultanas

5 glacé cherries, chopped

25g mixed peel, chopped

15ml or 1 tbs single cream

175g plain chocolate

Line 3 baking trays with non stick paper. Melt the butter in a saucepan over a low heat, add the sugar and boil the mixture for 1 minute. Remove the pan from the heat and add all the remaining ingredients, except the chocolate, stirring well to mix. Drop the mixture in small, well-rounded heaps on to the prepared sheets, allowing enough room between each for the mixture to spread. Bake the biscuit rounds in the oven at 180C for 10 minutes until golden brown. Leave on the baking sheets for 5 minutes until beginning to firm up, then lift on to a wire rack and leave until cooled. Break the chocolate into a heatproof bowl and place over simmering water. Stir until the chocolate is melted, then remove from the heat and leave to cool for 10 – 15 minutes. Just as the chocolate is beginning to set, spread it over the backs of the biscuits. Draw the prongs of a fork across the chocolate to make wavy lines and leave to set.

Pineapple wedges with rum butter glaze

Serves 4-6

1 medium pineapple

2 tbs dark sugar

1 tsp ground ginger

4 tbs melted butter

2 tbs dark rum

Cut pineapple lengthways into 4 or 6 wedges. Discard centre core. Cut between the flesh and skin to release the flesh, but leave the skin in place. Slice the flesh across into chunks. Push bamboo skewer lengthways through each wedge and into the stalk to hold the chunks in place. Mix together the sugar, ginger, melted butter and rum and brush over the pineapple. Cook the wedges on a hot barbecue for 3-4 minutes, pour the remaining glaze over the top and serve.

Fruit filled brandy baskets

Serves 2-4

50g margarine

60g caster sugar

2 tbs golden syrup

40g plain flour

1 level tsp ground ginger

1 tsp brandy

Finely grated rind of 1/2 a lemon

Fresh fruit to fill - strawberries, kiwis, mangos etc

Mint leaves to garnish

200ml cream

Melt the margarine with the sugar and syrup in a small pan over a low heat. Remove from the heat and stir in the sifted flour and ginger, brandy and lemon rind. Drop 1 teaspoon of the mixture about 4 inches apart from another teaspoon full (2 on one baking tray). Cook for about 7 minutes until bubbly and golden. Allow to cool for 1 minute then loosen with a palette knife and put on top of an upside down tumbler glass. Mould softly into shape. They can be all different sizes. Fill with fruit and then put 1 dessertspoonful of cream on top, followed by a whole strawberry and a piece of mint.

Avocado salsa

Serves 2

1 whole ripe avocado

1 tomato, finely chopped

1 small onion, finely chopped

2 bunch fresh coriander, chopped

2 tbs olive oil

Juice from 1 whole lemon

Salt and freshly ground pepper

Mix the chopped tomato, onion, olive oil and lemon juice together. Slice avocado and put on top of lettuce – spread the tomato and onion mixture on top. Sprinkle with chopped coriander.

Migration Camp

The cool blue of Migration Camp's lagoon swimming pool, set on a rocky terrace overlooking the Grumeti river, is a welcome sight among the harsh, sun-dried terrain of the western Serengeti. Migration Camp is built of gnarled timber and quarried stone, built into the hillside and facing the sunset. The camp's twenty green canvas tents all face the river, and are just another part of the bush to the hippo, wildebeest and lion that wander among them at night.

The dining area is a wooden terrace, with chunky furniture and wrought-iron fittings under a huge makuti thatch roof. Lunch is served next to the ice-cool pool, with wild fig trees growing through the dining terrace and rock hyraxes scuttling across the wooden deck. In the evenings, bush banquets take the dining experience to the wilderness, with a roaring campfire and long trestle tables set up in a clearing close to the river, the eyes of bushbabies reflected in the lamplights as they gaze down on the scene. Dinner is served with a flourish, as broadly grinning waiters arrive with domed silver food covers, removing them on the count of three and clashing them together like a dinner gong…

Fish in pastry

Serves 2

200g fish

5g butter

1 lemon

Seasoning

For the pastry

225g flour

175 pastry margarine, margarine or butter

1 egg

Pinch of salt

Sieve the flour and salt. Cut chilled butter into small cubes and lightly mix into flour. Roll the dough into a rectangle. Give one single turn, cover and allow to rest in a refrigerator. Give 3 more turns, allowing to rest between each. Allow to rest before using.

Pan fry fish and then fold with pastry for 1 to 2 minutes, transfer to baking tray, brush with beaten egg and bake at 220C for 20 minutes. Fold fish with pastry, transfer to baking tray, brush with beaten egg and bake at 220C.

Pumpkin soup

Serves 2

15g margarine or butter

100g onion, roughly chopped

200g pumpkin

100g potato

850ml stock - white chicken stock

Cook onion, potato and pumpkin until soft but not brown. Add the stock and bring to the boil. Simmer until cooked - about 30 minutes. Stir occasionally. Skim as necessary. Liquidize. Add a little more chicken stock if it is too thick.

Chicken stew

Serves 1

1 chicken breast

2 cloves garlic

1 medium onion

15ml oil

30g grated cheese

15ml oregano

1 big tomato

150ml stock

50g cooked rice

Cook onion until soft. Add chicken then garlic. Add tomato then stock and bring to the boil. Simmer for about 15 minutes. Stir in grated cheese. Serve with rice.

Aubergine salad

Serves 2

2 medium aubergines – sliced

30 ml sunflower oil

1 large tomato, skinned, deseeded and chopped

Seasoning to taste

Heat the oil and fry the aubergine. Arrange on the plate garnish with chopped tomato.

Tarangire National Park

During Tarangire's dry season, day after day of cloudless skies seem to suck all moisture from the landscape, turning the waving grasses to platinum blonde, brittle as straw.

Herds of elephant three hundred strong dig in the damp earth of the riverbed in search of underground springs, while wildebeest, zebra, buffalo, and gazelle mingle with rarer species such as eland and oryx around each shrinking lagoon. Python climb into the shade of the trees that line Tarangire's massive southern swamps and hang there, like giant malignant fruit, coils neatly arranged over the branches in a perfect sphere.

Tarangire's huge herds of elephant rival the park's gigantic, squat baobab trees as its most celebrated feature - ancient matriarchs, feisty young bulls and tiny, stumbling calves are ever present to fascinate visitors with their grace, intelligence and power.

Tarangire's vast wilderness zone, a part of the park many casual visitors never even dream exists, is a paradise for walking safaris, the only form of tourism allowed in this precious southern region. Visitors can explore the rivers, swamps and plains of this huge slice of wild Africa on foot, camping by night in fly-tents pitched under shady trees or next to waterholes, and learning skills, such as tracking and stalking, that most of mankind has long forgotten.

Kikoti Camp

Much of the décor at Kikoti Camp, a retreat of just ten tents in a private game conservancy of over 20,000 acres, is influenced by the design tradition of the Maasai people to whom this land belongs. Pretty beadwork necklaces hang on the walls of the bar, and spears are placed upright in earthenware pots next to the huge carved warriors who guard the entrance. Maasai shukas - bright red squares of blanket, checked or striped, which are worn by both warriors and elders - are used as tablecloths and napkins in the pleasant, shady dining room.

Shukas are also draped over the safari tables for dinner in the boma - a Maasai cattle enclosure created by placing jagged lengths of wood upright in the ground or dragging thorn bushes into a circle to keep out lion and other predators. The boma at Kikoti, however, has a different purpose - to serve as a venue for convivial dinners, with cutlery twinkling in the light from a roaring fire in the centre of the enclosure, and the moon rising to wink through the gaps in the tall wooden fence. Dinner in the Maasai boma is accompanied by singing and dancing from Kikoti's Maasai staff, many of who come from the local village from whom the camp's land is leased.

Wash and drain the fillet, dry on a clean kitchen cloth, cut into portions. Marinate the fillet with salt, pepper, lemon juice, chopped dill and few dashes of Worcester sauce. Leave the fillet to marinate for at least 1 hour. Dust the fillet on flour and pan fry. Make a thick sauce from the honey and orange juice, and dip the fried fillet in this sauce. Garnish with a small bunch of dill and lemon wedges.

Cream of spinach soup

Serves 4

150g butter

400g onions (finely chopped)

1.2kg spinach, chopped

300g flour

1l white stock

5dl fresh cream

1l milk

Salt & pepper

Heat the butter, add the onions and glaze slightly. Add the chopped spinach and cook slightly without changing colour for 5 minutes. Keep on a low heat for a short time and stir. Add the stock, bring it to boil, add salt and pepper and boil for about 20 minutes. Mix milk with flour, add and simmer for 30 minutes. Strain the soup through a straining cloth, put back to boil. Add spinach brunoise. Add the cream, taste and correct seasoning, serve.

Fish escallopines

Serves 4

1.6kgs Tilapia fish fillet

100g flour

125g butter

4 tbs lemon juice

Orange juice

Honey

A bunch of dill

Salt and pepper

Avocado vinaigrette

Serves 1

1 avocado

1 onion, chopped

1 cucumber, chopped

1 stick celery, chopped

1 tsp honey

1 tbs vinegar

Salt and pepper

Mix the ingredients. Peel the avocado, cut it into fingers and present on a side plate.

French onion soup

Serves 3

1 kg sliced onions

20g butter or margarine

1l white stock

4 slices of toast bread

60g cheese, grated

Prepare the onions and all the ingredients. Heat the butter in a small pan, fry the onions until brown. Add the white stock and cook for 20 minutes. Taste and correct seasoning. On serving, garnish the soup with toast and cheese.

Pepper steak

Serves 4

1kg fillet steak

20g butter

1 tbs black pepper

1 tsp ginger powder (paste)

1 tsp garlic powder (paste)

2 tbs olive oil

Mix all the ingredients and marinate the beef. Heat the butter in a frying pan until a blue haze rises from the pan. Season the steak with salt and pepper. Fry the steak briskly on the both sides. The cooking time depends on the thickness of the steak and on degree to which the steaks are cooked. Remove the steaks from the pan and arrange them neatly on a flat plate. Place a small bunch of parsley on the side.

Naitolia

Naitolia is a tiny eco-lodge nestling unobtrusively into the acacia and baobab trees that stand at the edge of the Lemiyon Plains, a vast expanse of waving, waist-high grasses that stretch away across the Tarangire Conservation Area. Herds of zebra, often accompanied by impala and giraffe, move peacefully around the edges of the camp, while a dazzling variety of birds flutter in and out of the open-sided buildings or perch in trees outside.

Naitolia has just four rooms, with low stone walls topped by sweet-smelling dry grass roofs, and open fronts to allow a view out across the plains from the cedar four-poster beds. The lodge also has one bedroom raised on stilts next to a vast old baobab tree and furnished with an enormous wrought iron double bed, from which elephants are sometimes visible as they come to drink at a nearby waterhole. Bathrooms are open air and surrounded by dried-grass screens. Hot water is brought in to gush from suspended canvas bucket showers, allowing guests the enjoyable experience of birdwatching while bathing!

Naitolia's emphasis is on the use of organic natural materials and traditional building methods, which gives the dining room as well as the bedrooms a relaxed, rustic charm. Food is cooked slowly over wood fires and served by candlelight, or eaten out in the bush next to a roaring fire.

Chicken in puff pastry

Serves 4

4 boned chicken breasts

Enough puff pastry when rolled to cover a 20cm square area per breast

50g grated mozzarella or gouda cheese per breast

4 small cloves of garlic

Coriander and mixed herbs

Stuffing: Prepare the ingredients by crushing one small clove of garlic, mix this with the grated cheese, a dash of coriander and mixed herbs to taste. Roll out the puff pastry into a square of about 20cm. Place the chicken breast in the centre of the puff pastry and stuff with the mixture; fold the puff pastry completely over the chicken breast and stuffing until completely sealed.

Place the chicken in puff pastry within the camp oven, and cover with a lid. Surround the camp oven with hot coals, making sure the bottom is only of medium heat. Ensure that the coals are also placed on top of the camp oven. Cooking time is about 40 minutes, or until the pastry has turned golden brown. Leave to cool before refrigerating. Slice into 5cm servings just before serving and eat hot or cold.

Roast leg of lamb

Serves 6

For this you will need a traditional cast iron camp oven or pot with a lid forming a tight seal.

1 medium sized leg of lamb

About 10 small garlic cloves

Whole bay leaves

10 small to medium sized wash potatoes

5 small onions

5 whole carrots, peeled

60ml cooking oil

Place small incisions in the leg of lamb and stuff with the whole garlic cloves and bay leaves. Rub the lamb with the oil and place the remaining in the camp oven or large cast iron pot. Wash the potatoes but leave the skin on, wash and peel the carrots and prepare the onions to be cooked whole. Place the leg of lamb, onions, potatoes and carrots into the camp oven. Place the lid on the camp oven or cast iron pot ensuring a tight seal.

Prepare a fire a whole 1/3 larger than the camp oven or cast iron pot. Place a layer of hot coals on the bottom of the hole, and then the camp oven or pot on top, surround the camp oven or pot with hot coals, including on the top. Cooking time is about 2 hours. When ready, carefully remove the lid and place the lamb on a serving platter surrounded by the potatoes, carrots and onions.

Serve hot with salads and gravy to suit.

Stuffed fillet steak in mushroom sauce

Serves 1-2

1 fillet of beef

50g grated mozzarella or gouda cheese

1 small clove of garlic

Mixed herbs

500g button mushrooms

2 medium onions, diced

200g cream

Stuffing: Prepare the ingredients by crushing one small clove of garlic, mix this with the grated cheese and mixed herbs to taste. Slice the fillet steak lengthwise and fill with the prepared stuffing, 'stitch' the steak together with toothpick or kebab sticks to seal. For the mushroom sauce, wash and peel the mushrooms. Cut and dice the onions. Add the cream and stir until the mixture thickens.

Place the steak into a medium size frying pan over medium hot coals. Cooking time between 15 and 35 minutes depending on taste.

For the mushroom sauce, fry the mushrooms and onions slowly until starting to brown then add the cream and stir continuously until the mixture starts to thicken.

Once the fillet is cooked, place on a serving platter and pour over the hot mushroom sauce just before serving. Serve with vegetables and potato croquettes.

Cold cooked lemon fillet of fish with potato skin chips

Serves 1-2

1 medium sized fish fillet

About 8 fresh lemons (or extract of lemon juice)

3 spring onions

About 10 small round potatoes

Cooking oil

1 tbs butter

Squeeze the lemons until enough lemon juice is available to completely cover the fillet of fish. Place the fish into a sealed container and pour over the lemon juice. Leave for about two hours. Lemons or limes can be used to cook the fish cold, and after a while the fish will start to turn white. The fish will also be marinated in the lemon juice and will have a slight lemon taste.

Slice the green leaves of the spring onions into about 3 cm long pieces. Wash the baby potatoes (do not peel) and slice into 3mm ellipses, place in cold water for 10 minutes, then drain.

Heat up the cooking oil until hot and cook the chips until they blister. The fish fillet should already be cooked; it is just a matter of taking from the container and sealing both sides quickly in a hot frying pan preferably with butter rather than oil. Serve on a bed of shredded lettuce, with the potato skin chips and cherry tomatoes.

Oliver's Camp

Recently relocated to the remote southern reaches of the Tarangire National Park, Oliver's Camp is run by Paul Oliver, one of Tanzania's top safari guides, and his wife Tati. The seven traditional bedroom tents are spread out far apart from each other along an acacia-clad ridge, allowing guests the feeling of freedom and space that is the essential component of any safari. The mess and dining tent is an open-sided, relaxed area, furnished with comfortable chairs and sofas for reading or birdwatching during the long hot afternoons.

Oliver's Camp is elegant and stylish, but unpretentiously designed to provide pleasant and atmospheric surroundings for the real purpose of any visit - a true wilderness experience. Guests are encouraged to leave their vehicles behind and walk through the park for at least part of their stay, learning as they do about all too easily forgotten details such as grasses, insects, birds and reptiles, and learning bush skills such as tracking and stalking from Paul himself or one of the camp's other expert and inspirational guides.

At the end of each day, the Oliver's team are quick to provide guests with all the comforts that the old-fashioned white hunters considered essential for their well-heeled clients - a fine wine cellar, catching the evening light as it lies in a wooden rack; ice clinking in a cold gin-and-tonic; and finally, a formal candlelit dinner, with safari stories flying around the table as the moon rises over the surrounding plains.

Orange soufflé

Serves 6-8

2 tbs fresh orange zest

120ml fresh orange juice

2 tsp gelatine powder

100g caster sugar

150g sweet biscuits crushed

4 eggs, separated

2 tbs melted butter

1/2 tsp cinnamon

Brush a 20cm round spring form tin with melted butter and line the base with non-stick baking paper. Put the biscuits in a food processor and crush finely. Stir in cinnamon and melted butter until all the crumbs are moistened. Press the biscuit mixture into the base of the tin and refrigerate for 10 minutes. Boil the juice for 5 minutes then stir in the gelatine and beat well until gelatine is dissolved. Beat egg yolks and sugar until light and fluffy. Then mix together with orange mixture in one bowl. In another bowl, beat the egg white with electric beaters or whisk until stiff peaks. Put in the orange zest and mix well. Pour into the orange mixture and mix well. Pour the mixture into the biscuit tin and chill in the refrigerator for 3 to 4 hours before serving.

Fish cakes

Serves 6

450g white fish fillets

3 tbs cornflour

1 tbs fish stock

1 egg lightly beaten

50g fresh coriander leaves

1 - 2 red chillis, chopped (optional)

3 tbs red curry paste

100g green beans very finely sliced

3 onions finely chopped

120ml oil

Sweet chilli sauce to serve

Process the fish in a food processor for 20 seconds until smooth. Add the cornflour, fish sauce, beaten egg, coriander, red chilli and curry paste. Process for 10 seconds or until well combined. Transfer the fish mixture to a large bowl. Add the beans and spring onions and mix well. Using wet hands, form 2 tablespoons of mixture at a time into flattish patties. Heat the oil in a heavy based pan over medium heat, cook 4 fish cakes at a time until golden brown on both sides. Drain on a paper towel and serve immediately with some chilli sauce.

Moroccan chicken

Serves 6

75g raisins

1/2 glass sherry

(Combine above in small bowl and set aside)

3 tbs butter

50g chopped onions

3 tbs flour

2 tbs curry powder

500ml milk

1 apple cored and sliced

1 tsp salt

6 boneless chicken breasts

20g sliced almonds

Sauté onions in butter until soft. Stir in flour and curry powder and cook for 2 - 3 minutes. Whisk in milk and bring to the boil. Add raisins, sherry and apples. Add salt to taste. Place chicken in a greased baking dish in a single layer. Pour sauce over and sprinkle almonds on top. Bake in a medium oven for about 30 minutes. Serve with coconut rice or plain rice.

Beetroot salad

Serves 4-6

300g chopped pineapple

500g chopped cooked and peeled beetroot

2 pieces cleaned and thinly sliced leeks

25g chopped black olives

2 tbs honey dressing

Place beetroot in a serving plate. Layer the top with pineapple and leeks and lastly, sprinkle olives (green or black (optional)) and then drizzle salad dressing on top.

Swala Camp

wala's resident manager and chef, Cindy Dennis, knows that when it comes to giving her guests a dramatic mealtime experience, she's got a lot to compete with. For breakfast, lunch and dinner at Swala camp are attended by a set of rather rowdy, but welcome guests - the twenty or so teenage bull elephants who often stroll up to gaze inquisitively into the dining room. Add to this the waterbuck and impala that wait politely behind the elephant for their turn to drink at the camp's waterhole, plus the pride of lion who often slope in just as dessert is being served, and Swala's guests could be forgiven for not giving their food the attention it deserves.

The menu at Swala, however, is enough to distract even the most avid wildlife watcher. Cindy believes that to serve up a truly memorable culinary experience, a chef has to remember the rule that 'people eat first with their eyes'. Her dishes are presented artistically and imaginatively, works of art on the plate that taste every bit as good as they look. Flexibility is key - out in the bush, ingredients have to be kept simple, and a sense of courage and experimentation prevails in the kitchen, with results just as dramatic and successful as the wildlife events in the bush outside.

Decadent chocolate mousse cornets

serves 4

Chocolate Mousse

250g dark chocolate

3 eggs

60g castor sugar

2 tsp dark rum

250ml cream

Melt the chocolate over boiling water, once melted and smooth, set aside to cool. Whip the eggs and sugar together until thick and pale. Whip cream until soft peaks form, and fold melted chocolate into the eggs alternating with the cream & rum. Pour into the cornets and place in refrigerator to set.

Chocolate cornets

300g dark chocolate

Cut triangles (a decent size) and twist to make a cornet. Secure cornet with a staple. Melt chocolate until smooth Spoon in dessert spoon of melted chocolate and smooth around cornet. Set in freezer.

To make up:

Pour mousse into set cornets and seal open end with chocolate. To serve, peel off wax paper and turn onto a flat bottomed dish, garnish with fruit and serve.

Summer tomato, basil & parmesan pasta

serves 4

500g fresh penne pasta

500ml water

1 can whole peeled tomatoes

1 can tomato puree (125g)

6 tomatoes

2 onions

1 green pepper

1 red pepper

1 bunch of parsley

1 clove of garlic

2 tbs olive oil

1 tsp wostershire sauce

A few drops tabasco sauce

2 tsp sugar

1 bunch basil for garnish

Fresh parmesan curls for garnish

Place water on to boil, add a touch of oil and salt. Bring water to boil and add pasta. Cook until *al dente* and drain.

To cook sauce:

Peel and chop onions and garlic clove and fry lightly in the olive oil. Add the chopped peppers, cook until tender. Add all the sauces and allow to sweat for 5 minutes. Add freshly chopped tomatoes, cook for 5 minutess. Add a can of tomatoes and tomato puree and allow to simmer and cook for 25 minutes. Season to taste. Place cooked pasta in a bowl and spoon sauce over pasta, garnish with fresh basil and parmesan curls.

Swala fruit kebabs with yoghurt dressing

serves 4

1/4 watermelon

1 punnet strawberries

1 small pawpaw (papaya)

1 small honey melon

1 small pineapple

4 kiwi fruit

Sauce

1 250ml tub of fruit yoghurt

50ml honey

5ml lemon juice

Peel and chop all the large fruit items into reasonable size squares, balls and wedges - leave strawberries whole. Place fruit, varying pieces, onto a kebab stick. Make the dressing by adding all ingredients together. Place kebab in a tall glass, drizzle with dressing and garnish with fresh mint.

Chargrilled Tarangire vegetable towers with balsamic dressing

serves 2

1 red pepper, chopped into large pieces

1 green pepper, chopped into large pieces

1 yellow pepper, chopped into large pieces

1 eggplant, sliced into thickish slices

1 zucchini, sliced into thick slices

1 tomato sliced

2 thick slices of mozzarella cheese

250ml balsamic vinegar

250ml olive oil

5ml tabasco sauce

1 tbs fresh chopped parsley

1 tbs freshly chopped basil

Combine all dressing ingredients in a large bowl and marinate the vegetables and cheese in the dressing for 1 - 2 hours. Cook vegetables on an open flamed fire until slightly singed. Keeping the dressing to one side, stack the vegetables and cheese and secure with a skewer. Bake in the oven until cheese has melted. Serve with the dressing and garnish with fresh herbs.

Tarangire Safari Lodge

Tarangire Safari Lodge, set high on a hill overlooking the park's permanent water source, the Tarangire River, is able to deliver one of the defining experiences of any safari - that of sipping a morning cup of tea or an evening sundowner while watching wildlife from the comfort of one's chair. The game drive circuits that surround Tarangire Safari Lodge can pall in comparison with an afternoon spent simply sitting, feet on the terrace parapet, binoculars in hand, scanning the magnificent vista of the valley below for the latest animal events while the smell of the evening's barbeque filters up from the kitchen and vervet monkeys lope past across the lawn.

Children in particular, often only tolerated in other safari lodges, enjoy the opportunity let off steam away from the cramped confines of a safari vehicle and splash around in the camp's pool, before returning to gaze out wide-eyed once again at the non-stop live action panorama of the Tarangire bush.

Rhubarb pie

Serves 4

200g butter (unsalted)

200g fresh rhubarb

250g icing sugar

10 ml vanilla essence

200g wheat flour

200g brown sugar

Mix icing sugar, wheat flour, butter and vanilla essence to make a dough then roll and lay on a round baking tray. Boil rhubarb for 5 minutes or until tender then mix the rhubarb with sugar. Pour the rhubarb on the pie dough. Use the remainder of the dough to cover the top of the pie. Bake for 20 minutes at 400F.

East African roast chicken

Serves 6

1 whole chicken

110g butter

1 tbs ground/mashed (fresh) garlic

1 tbs ground pepper

1 tbs tumeric

1/2 tbs cumin powder

2 tbs freshly copped coriander

4 tbs coconut milk

Mix all ingredients together with butter and ease skin of chicken away. Rub the marinade sauce generously all over the chicken. Chicken is ready for roasting.

Beef aubergine

Serves 6

500g beef steak

300g eggplant (cubed)

150g sliced onions

2 pieces beef cubes

4 tbs cooking oil

400g fresh tomatoes or 4 tbs tomato paste.

2 tsp fresh parsely

2 tsp black pepper

2 tsp salt

1 cup milk

Remove fat from beef (if any). Cut the meat into cubes and then cook with 2 cups of water for 25 minutes. Remove from heat and set aside. Take the sliced onions and fry until brown. Pour the tomato puree (or sauce from fresh tomatoes) into/ with the fried onions. Add the parsley, salt & pepper.

Add the uncooked eggplant to the meat sauce and cook for 10 minutes. Serve hot.

Marinated vegetable kebabs

Serves 4

Wedges x 8 for each of the following:

Pumpkin, onions, zucchini, bananas, aubergines, red pepper and green pepper

Marinade mixture:

4 tbs lemon juice

4 tbs cooking oil

4 tbs soy sauce

150 ml tomato juice

1/2 grated onion

3 crushed garlic cloves

1 tsp basil

1 tsp dried thyme

2 tbs butter

1 tbs fresh, chopped parsley

1 tsp black pepper

Blanch pumpkin wedges with aubergine wedges for 2 minutes. Mix together lemon juice, oil, soy sauce, tomato juice, grated onion, garlic and pepper and pour over all the vegetable wedges. Marinate for a few hours. Once the skewers are on the grill, baste the vegetable wedges again with the marinade sauce. Grill until golden brown.

Tarangire Treetops

The day at Tarangire Treetops begins when a soft creak of wood from outside heralds the ascent of the waiter, climbing the steps that lead to each elevated bedroom and calling 'good morning' softly before unzipping the canvas door flap. A slow, reluctant journey follows, out of the warm cotton quilts and across the smooth wooden floorboards to the tea tray placed by the window. The view, however, makes up for any hesitation about the chilly morning air - miles and miles of gently undulating landscape stretch away from each private treehouse, built into the crook of a giant baobab.

Breakfast is a hearty affair of eggs and bacon, fruit and muffins, served in the dining room, also built around a pair of massive baobab trees. By lunchtime, a group of elephant may have joined the party for a midday drink at the waterhole just below the terrace. At dinnertime, the enigmatic rustlings and squeakings that make up the sounds of the African night filter in through the open walls, and for an evening drink, the convivial bar, with its smart leather safari chairs and cream canvas cushions, is the perfect location to finish another day in this rather comfortable wilderness.

take a small spoon and drop spoonfuls of the mixture into the oil, frying until crispy and brown. Serve these with the shamba salad.

Cheese blinis

Serves 2

1 tsp baking powder

200g plain flour

200g grated cheese

250g breadcrumbs

1l oil for frying

4 eggs

500ml milk

Tarangire shamba salad with cheese balls

Serves 4

1 carrot, diced

1 baby marrow, diced

2 green peppers diced

2 tomatoes, cut in wedges

1 tsp mixed herbs

2 onions, cut in cubes

Cheese Balls:

50g flour

1 tsp baking powder

50g grated cheese

500ml oil for frying

1 pot cream

Pinch pepper

1 clove garlic

2 eggs

Mix all the dry ingredients in a bowl then add eggs and milk, stir to make a mixture. Form dough into rounded pancake shapes. Take the grated cheese put a teaspoon in the centre of each pancake and fold dough over to make a triangle shape. Roll each pancake in the bread-crumbs then deep fry until brown. Serve hot with

First boil carrots for a few minutes, then take a frying pan and cook onions till brown. Add mixed herbs and baby marrow, garlic, green pepper and pinch of pepper then finish with tomatoes. Cook for 5 minutes then add cream. **For cheese balls:** First put flour in a bowl then add baking powder, grated cheese and eggs. Stir together till all mixed then heat oil in a frying pan. Once hot,

kachumbari salad or salsa.

African beef kebabs
Serves 6

1 tomato, diced

1 baby marrow, diced

1 onion, diced

1 mango, diced

1 green pepper, diced

1 kg beef, cut into cubes

Garlic

Salt and pepper

Mixed herbs

You will also need kebab skewers for this recipe. Marinate your beef for at least 5 or 6 hours. Cut it into big cubes (about the size of ice cubes). Thread meat and vegetables onto the kebab sticks, alternating each ingredient. Grill over hot charcoal until brown. Serve with salad and cheese blinis.

Lemon meringue pie
Serves 6

1 box digestive biscuits

115g margarine or butter

Lemon juice

1 tin condensed milk

240ml egg white

1 tsp vanilla essence

Crush biscuits and butter together, then put in cooker and warm the mixture with cinnamon. Once warm, roll the mixture out flat. Take another bowl and mix condensed milk, vanilla essence and lemon juice, then pour this mixture onto the biscuit base. Put in fridge, while you whisk the egg white and sugar till stiff and firm. Put on top of biscuit and lemon mixture, bake in the oven for 20-25 minutes until brown. Serve.

Bib's Apple Special
Serves 2-4

1 tin apple slices

225g margarine

60g icing sugar

1 tsp baking powder

3 eggs

50g flour

120ml milk

1 tsp cinnamon

Arrange the sliced apple and cinnamon in a bowl, then melt butter or and leave to cool. Take icing sugar, baking powder, flour, milk and egg and mix together, then pour the cool melted butter into the mixture. Stir well, then put the mixture into the bowl of apple slices and bake for 15 minutes. Serve cold.

Lake Manyara

Stretched along the glittering, alkaline expanse of a Rift Valley lake, the Lake Manyara National Park is lower-key than some of Tanzania's other parks, but no less beautiful. Cool, lush mature fig forest grows up to the side of a huge, towering escarpment, tangled with creepers and with raptors circling overhead. Closer to the lake, the landscape widens out into floodplains on which herds of buffalo and wildebeest wander, sometimes seeking respite from the heat by wallowing in the salty water. Hot springs appear at intervals along the lake shore, the sulphurous water trickling out of the earth's core past slimy green rocks. Nearby, in shallow pools, dozens of hippo soak back to back, tails flicking and enormous mouths opening occasionally in cavernous yawns.

Lake Manyara National Park is famous for the huge herds of elephants, immortalised by the work of naturalist Iain Douglas-Hamilton during the 1970s. Poached badly in the 1980s, the elephant population has now recovered strongly, and are to be found in great herds along the dry riverbeds, or resting peacefully, calves between their legs, under trees in the heat of the day.

Lake Manyara Tree Lodge

Brought to fruition by South African architect Nick Plewman and interior designer Chris Browne, Lake Manyara Tree Lodge is a spectacular new safari lodge buried deep in the forest at the southern end of Lake Manyara National Park. The main lodge building is a soaring space built on multiple levels, and illuminated at night by dozens of lanterns.

Three exquisite meals daily - plus intermediate snacks - are served in the Lodge's boma-style ground level dining area, or in the upper dining room, a stylish space created entirely from wood, with bleached square tables that can be used as one, or broken apart to offer privacy. Thousands of beer bottles were melted down for transformation into the lodge's brown, bubbled glassware.

Each meal served at Lake Manyara Tree Lodge conforms to CC Africa's winning combination of new-age pan African cuisine, classic gourmet fare and comfort food. CC Africa aims to enrich the surrounding communities by using as much local produce as possible: at Lake Manyara, fiery watercress for salads comes from the nearby river, and the eggs from local farms.

Pears sangria

Serves 4

1 cup dry red wine

1 cup orange juice

1 orange/orange peel

1/2 a lemon/lemon peel

1 cinnamon stick

1 tsp vanilla essence

2 cloves (optional)

4 whole pears

Bring all ingredients to boil except the pears. Reduce heat then add the pears (without the juice). Simmer until tender (not soft), turning occasionally. Place pears and syrup in bowl, chill and serve with cream if desired.

Peach crumble

Serves 6

170g sugar

170g margarine

125g baking flour

1 1/2 tins peeled & sliced peaches

2 cups milk

1 tbs custard powder

Crumble together sugar, flour and margarine finely using the fingertips. Grease the baking tray. Take 1/2 of the crumbled mixture, place on the baking tray then place the peaches well drained on top. Finish off by placing the remaining mixture on top then press slowly with the palms. Bake in a preheated oven till start to turn brownish. Prepare the sauce by heating 2 cups of milk, then add 1 tablespoon of custard powder. Keep whisking continuously to avoid lumps forming. A smooth paste should be formed. Add sugar to taste.

Cucumber soup

Serves 6

3 cups water

500g milk

4 onions

5 pieces cucumber

3 tbs margarine

Salt & pepper to taste

Chop the onions and the cucumber. Heat the margarine. When ready add onions, fry till brown. Add all other ingredients, boil for 10 minutes. Take away from the fire and blend. Serve either warm or cold.

Lake Manyara orange & carrot soup

Serves 2

200g carrots

1l orange juice

1 tsp orange zest

1 clove garlic

1 tsp ginger

Salt & pepper to taste

500ml vegetable stock

Peel and slice the carrots, onions, garlic and ginger. Boil them with the orange zest and vegetable stock. Chop orange zest. Blend everything together. Add seasoning and a pinch of sugar. Strain to have a clear soup. Cool in the refrigerator, Serve cold.

Garlic yoghurt chicken

Serves 6

1 1/2 chickens

200 ml natural yoghurt

5 cloves crushed garlic

1 glass lemon juice

1 bunch finely chopped chives

1 tsp salt

1 tsp milled pepper

2 tsp honey

Mix all the ingredients to prepare a marinade and reserve. Wash and later pat dry the chicken then set aside. Preheat the grill. Place the chicken pieces on a grid of a roasting pan in the center of the oven till brownish. Then put under the grill for 6 minutes. Brush each chicken with the yoghurt marinade then grill for 5 more minutes. Turn over and repeat basting and turning process 2 more times. Serve hot.

Lake Manyara Serena

The flowing lines and bright colours of the Lake Manyara Serena's dining room, lounge and bar were inspired by the flocks of brightly coloured pelicans and flamingos that adorn the skies above the hotel. Perched on the edge of the Rift Valley escarpment, the Lake Manyara Serena looks down over the Lake Manyara National Park, and the great lines of birds that fly to and fro across the lake seem at times almost to float past at eye level. Their smaller cousins, vibrantly coloured sunbirds and starlings, rustle and chirrup constantly in the tropical gardens that surround the dining terrace, and swoop low across the lagoon swimming pool with its view of lake, sky and clouds.

The hotel is decorated in a vibrant combination of African colours, with decorative plasterwork patterns on the walls, bright tribal prints on the chairs and sofas and enormous basket-woven lights hanging from the ceilings. At breakfast, with the morning sun just beginning to warm the air, a buffet laden with delicacies from around the world - French pastries, Dutch pancakes or the traditional 'full English' - prepares guests for active days spent driving in the National Park, canoeing among the flocks of birds on the lake, or mountain biking along its shores.

Finely chop the white part of the leeks, put in a pan with the onion, stock and wine and simmer, covered, for 15 minutes or until very soft. Puree the mixture in a food processor, then pass though a sieve. Return to the pan and whisk in the yolks and cream. Whisk over low heat for 2-3 minutes or until slightly thickened - take care not to boil or it will curdle. Stir in the pine nuts. Cook the pasta *al dente*, pour the sauce over the top, and serve. Garnish with a handful of pine nuts.

Potato capsicum

Serves 4-6

500g potato, chopped into large cubes
1 tsp sesame seeds
Ginger paste
1 tsp cumin seeds
2 tbs chopped coriander leaves
1 big red and green capsicum
Oil for frying
1 tsp green chili paste
200g cashew nuts
3 tbs fresh or desiccated coconut

Machalari (stewed banana) with beef

Serves 4-6

10 green bananas (peeled and halved)
1 fresh beef fillet (cut into cubes)
250g red onion (thinly sliced)
1 fresh coconut (grated and make coconut milk)
3 fresh ripe red tomato (thinly sliced)
1 tbs corn oil
Salt

Boil the meat until it becomes tender. Fry onion with oil. Add the peeled tomato and cooked beef and its stock. Cook for twenty minutes until the banana becomes soft. Next add coconut milk and simmer for five minutes. Add salt for seasoning. Serve.

Pasta with leek and peanut sauce

Serves 4-6

200g leeks
1 onion, finely chopped
300ml chicken Stock
6 egg yolks
100ml cream
300g pine nuts, toasted and roughly chopped
Pasta of your choice

Wash, peel and cut the potatoes as for chips and deep-fry. Remove the core and seed from the capsicums. Cut them in long slices and deep-fry. Do not over fry. Drain the oil and keep on kitchen paper. Deep-fry the cashew nuts. In a heavy based saucepan, heat 2 table-spoons of oil and add cumin seeds and sesame seeds. When the spices begin to pop, add potatoes, capsicums, cashew nuts, lemon, juice, salt, chili paste and ginger paste. Cook for 5 - 6 minutes. Add coconut and coriander leaves. Garnish with cashew nuts.

Baked marble cheesecake

Serves 6

Base:

1 quantity shortcrust pastry

Filling:

1kg cream cheese

500g icing sugar

500ml milk

150g wheat flour

20g cocoa powder

Roll the pastry and line an 8 inch flan†tin or dish. Bake blind for 20 min-utes. Beat the cream cheese until smooth, then blend in the flour together with icing sugar and beaten eggs. Take half of the mixture above and pour into baked pastry. Cool for 10 minutes, then take the remaining mixture and add cocoa powder, and pour it on top. Bake the cake in the oven for 1 hour at 120C. Remove from the oven and cool for a few minutes. Garnish with icing sugar and serve.

Sokwe Mobile Camps

Sokwe is a safari outfitter specialising in providing mobile luxury camping safaris for Tanzania's top safari guides. The camps set up by Sokwe involve every kind of luxury, moved on the back of heavy lorries ahead of clients in their game-watching cars. Tents are vast, roomy affairs, with private verandahs and en-suite bathrooms, and guests dine at night in a magnificent formal mess tent, the long table carefully laid with glass and porcelain and illuminated by candlelight. Groups of family or friends hire the entire camp operation for themselves, making an old-fashioned private safari in the style of the glamorous days of the 1930s and 40s.

After a hard day's walking or driving in search of game, Sokwe's camps have the feel of an oasis of civilization and comfort in the midst of the bush. Not just comfort, but style is apparent in the decorative touches brought in from the surrounding countryside - rocks, dried grasses, seed pods and flowers adorn the tents and dining areas, their muted browns and golds matching the camp's green glass bottles, beige khaki and undyed canvas. Sokwe's camps, for all their style, are designed to blend in seamlessly with the surrounding colours of the bush and not stand out brashly against the natural beauty that invariably surrounds them.

for 15 minutes or until onion is soft. Add mangoes, rind and sugar and cook for one minute. Stir in the blended extra corn flour, water, stock cubes and lime juice. Bring to the boil stirring constantly. Reduce heat and simmer uncovered for 5 minutes. Serve chicken sprinkled with shallots and almonds.

Grilled green banana, cassava and sweet potato starter

Serves 2

2 green bananas, peeled and washed

Rub bananas in cooking oil , sprinkle with salt and grill until tender and well browned. Serve with coconut sauce.

2 sweet potatoes, peeled and washed

Cut into long thick strips, brush with cooking oil, sprinkle with salt and grill until tender and well browned. Serve with yoghurt and mango sauce.

2 pieces of cassava, peeled and washed

Cut into long thick strips, brush with cooking oil, sprinkle with salt and grill until tender and well browned. Serve with chachandu sauce.

Coconut sauce

1 small coconut, grated

1 tbs lemon juice

1 tbs fresh chopped coriander

2 tbs coconut milk

Salt and pepper to taste, pinch chilli powder

Combine grated coconut, lemon juice and coconut milk. Blend until thick. Add fresh chopped coriander, salt and pepper, pinch chili powder.

Yoghurt and mango sauce

1 ripe mango

3 tbs plain yoghurt

1 tbs lemon juice

1 tsp salt

Pinch black pepper

Combine all ingredients together and stir well.

Mango chicken with rice, steamed potatoes and sweet peas

Serves 4

2 tbs almonds

4 chicken breast fillets

2 tbs corn flour

15g butter

1tbs cooking oil

1 medium onion, finely chopped

2 cloves garlic, crushed

2 large mangoes, peeled and chopped

1 tsp grated lime rind

1 tbs castor sugar

1/2 cup water

1 small chicken stock cubes, crumbled

2 tbs lime juice

2 green shallots

2 tbs extra corn flour

Put finely chopped almonds on an oven tray in moderate oven for about 15 minutes. Cool. Cut each fillet into 4. Toss in corn flour. Heat butter and oil in frying pan. Add chicken gradually to pan in a single layer. Stir constantly over heat for 15 minutes or until chicken is well browned all over. Add onion and garlic to pan and cook

Chachandu sauce

2 ripe tomatoes peeled and seeded

1 onion, finely chopped

2 green chilies, finely chopped

2 tbs lemon juice

Salt and pepper to taste.

Blend tomatoes. Combine with remaining ingredients and stir well.

Pineapple and lime pie

3 1/2oz butter

6 oz digestive biscuits

2oz cashew nuts

For filling

1 tbs grated lime rind

5 fld oz lime juice,(juice 4 -5 large limes)

3 large egg yolks

14 oz condensed milk

6 oz chopped pineapple

To finish

Cream or plain yoghurt, lime slices. Loose-based flan dish, diameter 9 inches, 1 inch deep.

Put butter in a pan and melt over a low heat. Roast cashew nuts in oven and crush. Crush the digestive biscuits and mix with the cashew nuts. Add the melted butter and mix well. Put the mixture in the flan dish and press down evenly over the base and up the side of the dish. Bake in centre of a moderate oven until golden brown (10 minutes).

Whisk together the lime zest and egg yolks until the mixture has thickened. Add lime juice and mix again. Stir in the condensed milk and pineapple. Pour mixture over the biscuit base and return to the oven for about 20 minutes, or until set. Serve chilled with cream or yoghurt and a slice of lime.

Selous Game Reserve

A vast swathe of wilderness in the south of Tanzania, the Selous Game Reserve supports enormous numbers of animals in its 45,000 kilometre, unpopulated extent. The Selous is rightly known as one of Africa's most impressive wild places, and a destination for the true safari connoisseur. Once nicknamed Shamba ya Bibi (the wife's garden), the Selous was presented by Germany's Kaiser Wilhelm to his wife, and proclaimed a game sanctuary as early as 1905. The reserve takes its name from Frederick Courteney Selous, a heroic Victorian elephant hunter, naturalist, author and First World War captain, who died in 'The Battle for the Bush' here in 1917.

Across the breadth of the Selous meanders the great, muddy Rufiji River, teeming with huge crocodiles and pods of hippo. A boat trip is a highlight of any visit to the Selous, floating downstream past the tall, headless silhouettes of doum palms, on which fish eagles perch like figures on a totem pole. The Selous is famous for walking safaris and fly camping, giving visitors the chance to experience the adrenalin rush of watching elephant or lion on foot, or the unique tranquillity of sleeping under the stars in the predatory darkness of an African night.

Sand Rivers Selous

One of the greatest pleasures at Sand Rivers is to get up at dawn and spend the first hours of light messing about in a boat, chugging upriver as far as the steep-sided Stiegler's gorge then floating back down with the current, blinking at the million shades of green of the best-preserved riverine forest in Africa. Breakfast is fresh mango and bacon sandwiches, eaten on a shallow sandy beach as the sun gears up for the day's heat. A giant kingfisher flies by low over the water, and the grunts of hippo come startlingly close from behind a rock.

This sums up the dining style at Sand Rivers – meals can be arranged anywhere, from an island in the middle of the river to the magnificent formal dining room back at the lodge, where guests eat together around a huge table in the atmosphere of a private dinner party, the conversation convivial and the tall safari stories starting to flow.

The Sand Rivers team are young and obliging; just let them know if you fancy a candlelit dinner for two on a sandbank, or a day marooned on an island with a cool box and a radio, and they'll arrange it without a blink.

Cream cheese and fresh herb roulade

This cream cheese roulade is delicious to have on melba toast and to accompany soup for a light lunch or starter.

400g cream cheese
Green or black olives chopped
Handful peeled and roasted almonds, chopped
Chopped fresh parsley, chopped fresh oregano, chopped fresh thyme
Sweet paprika or spanish paprika
Salt and pepper
Cling film

Mix cream cheese chopped almonds and olives, season with salt and ground black peppercorns. Spread evenly in about 1cm thickness on a 30cm long piece of cling film placed on a shallow baking tray and leave in the fridge or freezer till slightly hardened. When hard, cover half the rectangle of cheese completely with the chopped herbs and the other half with sweet paprika. Grab one end of the rectangle of cling film and roll up. Wrap in cling film and leave in the fridge till serving. Before serving, sprinkle more fresh herbs and paprika on the top and cut a slice off the ends to make it even and tidy. You will see the swirls of red and green in the rolled up cheese.

Mama's banana cake

3 mashed bananas
100g butter
1 cup white sugar
1 cup white flour
1 egg
1/2 tsp salt
1/2 tsp bicarbonate of soda

Butter a medium cake tin. This cake is very easy to make and is more delicious when mixed by hand and not with electric beaters or mixers. Cream butter, add sugar slowly beating well with a wooden spoon. Add egg, salt, mashed bananas, sift in flour and bicarbonate. Bake in a moderate oven for 45 minutes till golden brown but slightly sticky on top. The cake will not rise, in fact it may even dip a little in the middle. But it is all the more delicious for having a mushy middle! Sprinkle with icing sugar when cool.

Quick and painless pastry and tomato tart

Serves 6

A good option if you are bored with the traditional quiche!

Pastry:

225g white flour (plain)

150g butter or margarine softened

1 egg yolk mixed with 4 tbs water

1 tsp salt

1 tbs icing sugar

Filling:

2 small onions finely chopped

4 cloves garlic finely chopped

1 tbs olive oil

400g (one tin) tomato paste or puree. If tins not available or only concentrate available, puree 5 ripe tomatoes after removing skins by dropping in boiling water for 1 minute. Peel then process the mixture adding 1 table-spoon of tomato concentrate.

3 tsp sugar

3 tbs grated cheddar cheese

3 eggs

Shallow flan dish or pie case

To prepare pastry: (delicious for other sweet or savoury fillings also)

If you have a food mixer process butter, flour, salt and sugar till crumbly. Slowly pour in egg yolk mixed with water till mixture forms a ball, then stop immediately. Turn out onto a floured board and roll out till 3mm thickness and line the pie case. Leave in the fridge to rest for 15 to 20 minutes and then bake blind in preheated oven for 15 minutes.

To prepare tomato filling:

In a heavy bottomed saucepan cook put the olive oil, onions and garlic and cook until soft, then add tomato paste, sugar. Cook stirring for 10 minutes till it boils.

Put aside to cool.

Bake pastry in slow oven for 10 minutes (it must not be brown or crisp). Add the cheese and eggs to the tomato paste filling, mix well and pour into pastry. Decorate with olives around the edge and cook slowly in a medium oven for 15 minutes.

Can be served warm or cold.

Selous Safari Camp

Selous Safari Camp is an extremely elegant tented camp, true to the authentic style of the safaris of the Victorian era. The camp is spread out through a patch of woodland right at the edge of the Rufiji River, offering stunning views from its dramatic dining room-cum-bar, raised on stilts to see far out over the water. Inside, elegant colonial furniture adds to the period feel of the camp, with various more local decorations such as canoe paddles and dried acacia fruit adding African flavour. Sofas, armchairs and *chaises longues* are provided, together with several bookcases full of informative safari literature, for guests who'd like to while away a long hot afternoon. The area's many varieties of brilliantly coloured birds swoop in and out constantly, and binoculars and field guides are also provided in the mess area for armchair ornithologists!

Early each morning, a beautifully laid wooden tea tray appears on each tent's verandah, complete with brass milk jug, bamboo tea cosy. In the evening, hurricane lamps are hung around the great dining structure, casting a warm orange glow over the convivial dining tables, at which an innovative and eclectic menu is served, followed by fresh coffee, tea and homemade biscuits.

Stuffed Chinese cabbage rolls on ginger egg noodles

Serves 3

6 large green leaves from Chinese cabbage

1 large red pepper

1 large yellow pepper

3 tsp black sesame seeds (black poppy seeds can be substituted)

300g rice

2 tsp sesame oil

240ml coconut milk

3 spring onions (chopped)

3 tbs cream

1 tsp ginger

1 packet egg noodles

Chutney to serve

Vegetable oil for deep frying

Batter:

700ml water

2 large eggs

3 tbs flour

1 tsp kudzu (Japanese root used for tempura and found in health stores)

Blanch the large leaves of the Chinese cabbage in boiling water and allow to cool - open up the leaf when cool-

ing. Slice the red and yellow pepper in long thin sticks. Boil the rice in coconut milk, when cooked toss with black sesame seeds (or black poppy seeds). On the flat open Chinese cabbage leaf put a thin layer of rice to cover the lower centre of the leaf. Top with the pepper sticks then cover with more rice. Roll the leaf sideways and seal by tucking in each end of the leaf into the actual roll. For the batter combine the flour, egg and 1 tsp kudzu (which should be diluted in 1/2 tea cup of water -put into fridge and chill well). Boil the noodles in a little water, drain and allow to cool. Toss with grated ginger, cream and sesame oil. Preheat the oil in a wok or deep frying pan. Take one roll and cover completely with the cold batter. Submerge in very hot oil turning slowly and cook for approximately 5 minutes until light golden brown. Remove from oil and slice in half immediately while hot. Place 2 rolls on a bed of egg noodles. Sprinkle with chopped spring onion and serve with a dollop of mango chutney on the side of a plate.

Sliced mango and red onion salad with basil vinaigrette

Serves 2

1 mango

1 red onion

1 red pepper

Fresh basil leaves

4 tbs olive oil

4 tbs balsamic vinegar

Vinaigrette:

1 tsp white vinegar

1 tbs mayonnaise

6 basil leaves chopped finely

1 tbs whole grain mustard

Salt to taste

Roast the red pepper until the outside skin is blackened. Soak in water until soft and peel the black skin off until left with the red pepper meat. Remove the pepper seeds and slice 2cm strips. Then marinade the pieces in olive oil and balsamic vinegar (these can be kept in the fridge in a jar for weeks). Slice the mango and red onion thinly and layer harlequin style on a small plate. Place 2 fresh basil leaves between the mango and onion slices. Drizzle the dressing over and garnish with the roasted red pepper slices. Serve chilled.

Red snapper in orange with fennel and sundried tomatoes

Serves 3

1 kg red snapper fillet
240ml fresh orange juice
A few slices of fresh orange
1 tbs fennel seeds (crushed)
500g butter
3 sundried tomatoes
Sprigs of fresh dill

Marinade the red snapper fillets in the fresh orange juice for 3 - 4 hours in the fridge. In a frying pan heat the butter, add the crushed fennel seeds and sundried tomatoes. Remove the sundried tomatoes and sauté the fish fillets until cooked through but still tender. Garnish with orange slices and sundried tomatoes. Serve immediately with a sprig of fresh dill.

Date and coconut pudding

Serves 6

175g dates (pitted and chopped finely)
1/2 tsp bicarbonate of soda
1 cup boiling water
1 large egg (beaten well)
150g flour
1 tsp vanilla essence
225g white sugar
55g butter

1 tsp baking powder
Pinch of salt
Cream for serving
Mint leaves for garnish
Syrup ingredients:
225g sugar
75g freshly grated coconut (or desiccated coconut)
6 level tbs butter
4 tbs milk

Heat the oven to 180C. Cut the dates finely. Put the dates in a bowl and pour the bicarbonate of soda and the boiling water over the dates. Leave for about 20 minutes until the dates are soft and a thick mixture is formed. Cream the butter and sugar together, add the egg and then add the dry ingredients, vanilla essence and the date mixture. Pour into a big greased casserole dish and bake in the oven for approximately 1/2 an hour. Remove from the oven. In a pot add all the ingredients for the syrup until sugar is melted and syrup is hot. Pour over the warm pudding. Return to the oven for a few minutes. Cut into squares, serve with a dollop of cream on top, and garnish with mint leaves.

Ruaha National Park

Ruaha National Park is Tanzania's second largest, a vast wilderness in the south-west of the country visited by only a handful of travellers each year. At the park's heart is the aptly-named Great Ruaha River, a massive watercourse that dwindles to only a few pools in the dry season, but bursts its banks and roars over boulders at the height of the rains.

Converging with the Great Ruaha are hundreds of sand rivers, natural game corridors when dry and sparklingly clear streams when wet. Waterbuck, impala and the world's most southerly Grant's gazelle risk their lives for a sip of water - the shores of the Ruaha are a permanent hunting ground for lion, leopard, jackal, hyena and the rare and endangered African wild dog. Ruaha's elephants are recovering strongly from ivory poaching in the 1980s and remain the largest population in East Africa. Ruaha represents a transition zone where eastern and southern species of flora and fauna overlap - lesser and greater kudu co-exist with northern species such as Grant's gazelle.

Between the rivers lies a massive, completely unspoilt landscape of plains, rocky gullies, thick miombo woodland and distant purple hills. Ruaha is a dramatic park, its scenery ever-changing and full of detail - the white blossoms that appear on the bald, stark branches of baobab trees, the gigantic blue-black granite boulders that lie in tumbled plains in the river valleys, and the cloudy springs that bubble up in green, pungent swamps.

Jongomero

Jongomero, the newest camp in Ruaha National Park, comprises a series of open sided mess buildings and canvas tents built overlooking the Jongomero river, a tributary of the massive Ruaha River. The Jongomero is dry for six months of the year, forming a natural game corridor for impala and elephant, who come to dig for water in the sandy riverbed during the heat of the day.

Guests at Jongomero often take a packed breakfast with them on early morning game drives, stopping in the shade of a tree after a morning searching for the shy kudu and sable antelope and rare African wild dog that frequent the area of the camp. Cereal and fruit juice are enjoyed reclining on cushions on the ground, perhaps overlooking the glittering granite boulders of the Ruaha riverbed and listening to the bubbling call of a dove from the surrounding bush.

Lunch is served on the river bed itself, with tables spread with colourful Maasai blankets under a spreading acacia tree. In the evenings, drinks are served on the stone flagged terrace of the bar as long bars of sunlight fall across the golden wood of the bar floor and shy impala appear on the opposite bank to graze. Dinner is taken under the massive straw roof of the dining room, the night sky ablaze with stars and the roar of Jongomero's resident lion pride echoing distantly through the darkness.

Lemon tart

Serves 6

250ml fresh cream

500ml milk

3 tsp lemon rind

4 tbs lemon juice

150g sugar

2 tbs gelatine

6 drops vanilla essence

2 eggs

Grease a 24cm round-based flan tin. Process flour, margarine and sugar until just crumbly. Add enough water to make ingredients just cling together. Press dough into a ball, knead gently on a floured surface until smooth, wrap in plastic and then refrigerate for 30 minutes. Roll the pastry between sheets of baking paper until large enough to line the tin. Lift the pastry into the tin then bake in a medium oven for 30 minutes.

For the filling:

Mix fresh cream, milk and sugar in a medium bowl until thick, then add lemon juice, lemon rind and egg. Bring to the boil, remove from heat and add gelatine and vanilla essence, then cool and pour into the tart base. Refrigerate for one hour and serve decorated with slices of lemon.

Mushroom pancakes with cheese sauce

Serves 5

For the pancake mixture:

200g flour

25g butter, melted

1 egg

Pinch salt

25ml milk

For the filling:

20g butter

2 medium onions, chopped

2 cloves garlic

2 tins chopped mushrooms

2 tbs cream

1 tbs cheese

For the cheese sauce:

25g butter

100g flour

250ml milk

100g cheese

Salt and pepper

Make the pancakes by mixing together all ingredients and cooking in a flat bottomed frying pan. Melt butter, sauté onions, garlic and mushrooms together for 2 minutes or until tender. Add cream and cheese and season. Make the cheese sauce by melting butter, then adding the flour and whisking together for 5 minutes. Add milk and leave to simmer for at least 15 minutes. Then add grated cheese, stirring continuously, and season to taste. Place a tablespoon of mushroom mixture into the centre of each pancake then fold the pancake around it into a triangle. Top with cheese sauce and garnish with vegetables.

Mini pizzas
Serves 6

500g flour

5g yeast

5g salt

25g butter

50g olive oil

5dl water

Onions, garlic, tomato, all chopped

1 tin tomato paste

Chopped vegetables - mushrooms, olives, peppers etc

Mix the ingredients together to form a dough. Roll out to 3mm thickness. Cut to required size - about 6cm in diameter. Simmer tomatoes, onions and garlic together with garlic paste and a little water for 10 minutes, then spoon the cooked mixture onto the dough circles. Add chopped vegetables and grated cheese and grill until just browned.

Beef stroganoff
Serves 6

1kg shredded beef

2 tbs oil

1 large onion

5 cloves garlic

1 small carrot

10g mushrooms

2 tbs tomato paste

2 tbs tomato puree

1l beef stock

Sauté shredded beef together with garlic and chopped onions. Add tomato paste and tomato puree then continue to sauté until brown. Add beef stock then leave to simmer for 20 minutes before adding chopped carrot, onions, green pepper and mushrooms. Serve with rice and steamed vegetables and garnish with grilled tomato.

Mwagusi Safari Camp

At Mwagusi Safari Camp, a tiny, discreet bush camp nestling into a bend in the Mwagusi river, the day begins with a dawn bird walk in the bush around the camp. Owner Chris Fox, justly famous throughout Tanzania as a safari guide, believes that his own bush skills, picked up over a lifetime spent exploring the Ruaha National Park, are best imparted on foot rather than solely in a vehicle. Returning to camp, Chris's guests are greeted by the warm crackle of a campfire in the still-chilly morning air, with ancient iron kettles propped onto the coals for morning tea.

After the morning's game viewing, driving out into the park to seek out a herd of elephant digging for water in a riverbed or a pride of lion resting in the shade of a rock, guests return for lunch around a long table in the camp's stylish dining banda, built of local stone and straw and decorated with natural objects such as skulls and branches found in the surrounding bush.

In dry season evenings, the dinner table is moved to the sandy riverbed that flows past the camp, with a huge campfire blazing alongside in the shelter of an overhanging rock. The camp's sumptuous dinner is sometimes interrupted by Constantine, a bull elephant who has enjoyed a lifelong friendship with Chris, looming out of the darkness in search of a morsel of his own. Few are likely to refuse!

Tomato bruschetta

Serves 4

6 ripe plum tomatoes
1/4 tsp castor sugar
1 tbs fresh chopped basil
4 slices of white bread
1 clove garlic
4 tbs olive oil
Salt and pepper
Basil springs to garnish

Peel and roughly dice the tomatoes, mix with the sugar, chopped basil, and two tablespoons of olive oil together in a bowl. Cover and set aside for half an hour. Toast the bread until crisp and golden brown, rub the sliced clove of garlic all over the bread. Spoon the tomato mixture onto the toast and press firmly into toast. Drizzle the remaining olive oil over and season with salt and pepper. Garnish with basil springs and serve.

Mango shortbread

Serves 6

250g flour
300g butter
100g sugar
250 ml cream
3 mangos
1 tbs brandy

Melt the butter. Then mix the flour and sugar with the melted butter and make a dough. Roll out the dough and cut with pastry cutter into 6 pieces. Bake in medium hot oven for 15 minutes until golden brown. Take the flesh of two mangoes and mash and add the brandy. Whip the cream and add 1 tablespoon of the whipped cream on top of the shortbread as a layer. Add 3 or 4 finely cut slices of mango in a fan shape on top of the whipped cream. Spoon the mango mixture around the edge of the plate to serve.

Spinach and chicken terrine

Serves 6

1kg spinach

1 medium sized chicken

1 whole garlic

1 tbs olive oil

1 tsp chopped fresh tarragon

Salt and pepper

Debone the chicken and slice into small strips. Boil the spinach with olive oil and garlic for 5 minutes. Layer the chicken and spinach alternately and sprinkle every second layer with tarragon. Continue layering using all the spinach and chicken. Place the baking tin in a hot oven for 15 minutes. Remove from tin and place on a bed of salad and decorate with finely sliced tomatoes.

Orange marmalade mousse

Serves 3

3 whole oranges

3 tbs orange marmalade

6 tbs single cream

1 tbs brandy

2 tbs icing sugar

Slice the top off the orange and hollow out the orange removing the pips from the orange flesh. Chop the orange flesh finely and mix with the icing sugar. Whip the cream until nearly hard and add the orange mixture. Then add the orange marmalade and brandy. Scoop the mixture back into the hollow orange, replace lid and decorate before serving.

Ginger beef

Serves 4

500g beef

300g carrots

200g onions

500ml orange juice

2 tbs honey

2 tbs soy sauce

3 tbs sesame seeds

3 tbs of grated ginger

1 clove of garlic

Salt

Boil the beef slowly with garlic and salt for one hour. Slice the onions into strips and fry until brown and crispy. Peel the carrots and slice into strips and boil for 5 minutes. Make a sauce from the orange juice, honey, soy sauce and sesame by mixing all together. Slice the boiled beef into strips and pour over the sauce and mix well. Garnish the beef with the carrot and onion strips and sprinkle with sesame seeds. Serve with egg fried rice.

Ruaha River Lodge

Overlooking a magnificent bend in the Ruaha River, the main artery of the vast Ruaha National Park, Ruaha River Lodge is a relaxed and unpretentious lodge built on two levels, with one section along the edge of the boulder-strewn riverbed, and another etched into the granite of the magnificent granite kopjes that tower up the banks.

Down by the river, the dining banda is a low-roofed, open sided room, with wading birds swooping down to drink from the water just yards in front of it, and shy antelope appearing from the surrounding bush to quench their thirst. Up among the kopjes at the main camp, the dining room has a bird's eye view of the river valley, with its surrounding purple hills and magnificent baobab and acacia woodlands. From here, scanning with binoculars, a myriad of sights jump into view - a giraffe bending slowly down to drink, legs splayed precariously, or one of Ruaha's huge herds of buffalo streaming like a black river through the bush on their way to the water.

In both camps, however, the food is equally satisfying - cooked mainly using fresh meat, vegetables and dairy produce from the owners' family farm in the highlands of Iringa, the menu includes fresh-baked cinnamon bread at breakfast, hearty sides of honey-glazed ham for lunch, and at after dinner, a richly hedonistic Amarula mousse.

Coffee and Amarula mousse

Serves 4

4 eggs

250ml double cream

1 tot Amarula

1tsp instant coffee

1 sachet gelatine

50g sugar

Separate eggs, whisk yolks with sugar until thick and creamy. Add Amarula. Dissolve gelatine and coffee in 1 tablespoon hot water and stir. Whisk egg whites until stiff, whip the cream, and stir the gelatine mixture into the egg yolks and sugar mix. Fold in the cream and egg white, reserving a little cream for decoration. Spoon into individual serving pots and refrigerate until set. Pipe whirls of cream on mousse and decorate with a coffee bean.

Cinnamon bread

Serves 4

1 quantity bread dough (use 250g flour)

50g butter

Powdered cinnamon to taste

1 egg, beaten

Roll out the dough to a rectangle half a centimetre thick. Melt butter and brush it over the dough. Sprinkle the sugar and cinnamon over the top. Roll up, Swiss roll style starting with the long side. Bend into a ring shape and place on a greased baking tray. Brush with beaten egg and bake in a hot oven for 35-40 minutes.

Globe artichoke with garlic hollandaise

Serves 4

1 globe artichoke per person

2 cloves garlic, minced

4 oz unsalted butter

2 egg yolks

2 tbs lime juice

Salt and pepper

Boil artichokes for 30-40 minutes, add a little vinegar to the water. Make sauce, melt butter and whisk egg yolks. Very slowly pour the butter onto the egg yolk, whisking all the time until emulsified. Add lime juice, garlic, salt and pepper. Serve with warm artichokes on the side.

Honey and mustard glazed ham

1 2-3kg ham

Handful of cloves

3 tbs honey

2 tbs mustard - homemade or English

Boil ham for 3 hours or until cooked. Remove from water and press the cloves into the outside. Mix together honey and mustard and brush generously over the ham. Bake in a hot oven for 20-30 minutes until brown..

Mahale National Park

Deep in the forest, with its trailing vines and tangled creepers, a high, shrieking hoot is heard, followed by a wild screaming and a deafening crash of branches. Suddenly a chimpanzee appears on the rock-strewn path, teeth bared defensively and massive shoulders hunched in aggression. This is the alpha male of the group, Fenana, making his presence felt to the fifty or so chimps that are presently feeding in this part of the forest. He breaks off a branch and charges, flailing the leaves wildly around his head in a wild display of power.

A young female with a baby appears suddenly from the undergrowth - as she joins in the grooming, her baby jumps down from his jockey-style position on her back and amuses himself turning somersaults and chasing the giant blue butterflies that flutter past in the shafts of sunlight that filter down through the trees.

Just another ordinary day for the Japanese research team who have been studying this group of chimpanzees continually since 1965. Thanks to their work the chimpanzees, while still 100% wild, are fully habituated to human beings, and can be joined in the forest by small groups of visitors, who make the steep climb up through the humid forest to the apes' domain.

Greystoke Camp

The chimpanzees who inhabit the Kasoge forest of Mahale Mountains National Park roam through their home range for miles each day, deftly plucking their day's diet from among the many types of wild fruits, nuts, leaves found in the woodland. The chimps expertly strip the leaves from twigs and use them to 'fish' for ants, poking them into treetrunks then nibbling off the insects as they emerge. A group of chimps will even occasionally surround a red colobus monkey or a young bushbuck, tearing it apart after a wild, shrieking chase and then gleefully sharing out the raw meat.

For the chefs at isolated Greystoke Camp, set at the edge of the forest on a pristine white beach on the shores of Lake Tanganyika, similar ingenuity is required in order to produce the eclectic, innovative cuisine for which the camp is famous (safari ants and raw monkey, however, are mercifully absent from the menu).

Fresh forest ginger is crushed with wild lemon to make a cooling ginger beer, served to grateful guests on their return from a long day in the humid forest on the trail of the chimps. Enormous, juicy freshwater mussels are gathered from the lake's bottom with a snorkel and fins, to be baked, topped with grated cheese and served at lunchtime in the camp's elegant palm-thatched mess. In the mornings, the kitchen takes to the beach, cooking up robust pre-trekking breakfasts of fishcakes and scrambled egg over a charcoal brazier on the sand.

Speke's moules champignon

Serves 6

6 Speke's mussels - larger the better (can be up to 20cm long)

1 medium onion

2 cloves garlic

30g dried mushrooms

150g fresh button mushrooms

80ml full cream

1/2 glass white wine

2 tsp light soy sauce

1 knob butter

100g cheddar cheese

Salt and pepper to season

Walk out across the beach to the lakeshore with mask, snorkel and flippers and a small string bag. Dive into the crystal clear waters of Lake Tanganyika. At the base of the rocks you'll find a deep sandy bed where these giant mussels lie. Gather a few and return to shore. (If you can't make it all the way to Lake Tanganyika, 20 ordinary mussels will do!)

Put the mushrooms in 300ml of warm water to soak for an hour. Clean the mussels and steam them until the shells are wide open. Remove them from their shells and cut off the hard section that attaches them to the shell together with the stomach area - a straight diagonal line, leaving 3/4 of the mussel flesh. Rinse this to remove any sand and chop finely.

Fry up the finely chopped onions and garlic in a knob of butter until lightly browned. Drain the soaked mushrooms, retaining the water. Now add these and the fresh mushrooms, also finely chopped, to the pan. Fry gently for 10 minutes, then remove from heat and add the white wine, soy sauce, cream and the chopped mussels. Season with salt and pepper to taste.

Place the empty shells on their back on a baking tray. You may have to twist and bend the join a bit to make them lie flat but be careful not to separate them. Now spoon the mixture into the shells, top with grated cheese and place in hot oven for 5 minutes until the cheese has melted. Serve immediately as a starter with freshly baked bread and butter.

Forest ginger beer

Serves 3

This will quench the thirst of the hottest of 'chimpers' as they return from their machete-wielding, primate-tracking expeditions through the forest. If you can find it, a few roots of wild African ginger and a handful of ripped ginger leaves grabbed while in the forest add an extra punch that sends the taste buds reeling.

300g ginger (or 250g ginger, 100g wild ginger root)
3 lemons
2 limes
5 tbs soft brown sugar
100ml spring water
1l soda water

Peel and grate the ginger. Scrub the lemons and limes to remove the waxy layer of the peel and then quarter them. Add the water and brown sugar and using a pestle, bash them together, squeezing the juice from the fruits so that all of the flavours combine. If you are using African ginger, rip a few leaves into the mixture. Leave it to marinade for an hour or so, ideally refrigerated. Then pass the mixture through a coarse sieve, squeezing the last of the juice from the mixture. Pour the concentrate over ice and top up with the litre of soda water. You may have to add more sugar or lemon juice to taste. Frost the rims of the glasses by dipping first into lemon juice, then soft brown sugar.

A shot of rum transforms this into a punchy cocktail - the *Lakuga*, named after the wind that brings dark and stormy nights to Mahale at the end of the dry season.

Peckish primate power bars

Serves 6

When you have been up since dawn and your full English breakfast has been burnt off from a morning tracking the chimps, these are the most welcome trail munchies imaginable and have (apparently) saved many lives.

225g butter or margarine

200g unrefined sugar

1 tbs honey

1 tbs black treacle (or another honey/golden syrup)

100g self-raising flour (or plain flour plus 2 pinches of bicarbonate of soda)

100g rolled white oats

Handful of raisins

1 tsp mixed spice

Heat the margarine or butter until melted with the sugar, honey and treacle. In a mixing bowl, put the oats in first and then sift in the flour. Add the raisins and mixed spice and mix all dry ingredients together thoroughly. Then mix in the melted mix until you get a large lump of mixture that only just binds together. If it is too sloppy, add another handful of oats.

Grease a baking tray (approx 30cm x 20cm) generously with butter. With your hands, push the mixture into the tray making sure that you squeeze it all right up to the edges and into the corners so you have one big flat layer about 1/2 cm thick. Bake in a moderate oven (gas 5) for about 14 minutes until just browning on the top. When you remove, it may appear too soft but it will set. Before it does, using a sharp knife, cut into 4 cm squares but leave it to cool in the baking tray. Once cool, the flap-jacks will lift out easily.

Mahale sashimi

Serves 8

For our sashimi we use the kuhe - the world's largest cichlid and present in abundance in the right season off the shores of Mahale. This delicate fish, when chilled and finely sliced is as good as any on the planet to eat raw - as certified by our Japanese friends on the chimpanzee study programme here.

500g suitable raw fish
30ml light soy sauce
Thumb sized piece of ginger
1 small lime (1 tsp juice)

Fillet the fish and slice thinly into strips. Pour the soy sauce into a small dish or ramekin. Grate the ginger and juice the lime, removing the pips, and add to the soy sauce, stirring well. Arrange the fish on a plate around the dip and serve with chopsticks.

If you freeze the fish it is much easier to slice it thinly which gives people the option to have a lot or a little. Freezing also will kill any harmful bacteria that may be present though if you are in any doubt as to the purity of your fish source you might think again. That is not something we worry about, often making sashimi right there on the dhow as we pull kuhe from the crystal waters. Try a good hit of wasabi to top the fish after dipping. Then, just as the rush hits the back of your nose, chase it with a chilled shot of Stolichnaya vodka, sit back and

Katavi National Park

Katavi National Park feels like the beginning of the world - an enormous primeval land in which the beasts still rule, far from the influence of mankind. Man is the minority here, and this is not his domain - it belongs instead to the vast herds of buffalo, roan antelope, and elephant, who seem to have inhabited this place since time began. Hippos in their hundreds pack into the dry-season pools and swamps, or wander across the flood plains in search of grazing. Crocodiles are here in vast numbers too, hiding in hollows in the river banks or sliding into the water in pursuit of fish.

The animals in Katavi seem somehow larger than life, bigger and more real than in other parks. Waterbuck are heavyset and deerlike, their shaggy coats reflecting the sunlight as they crop the lush green grasses that line the rivers and streams, fed by underground springs.

Walking is allowed, for a closer look at the innumerable birds that wade in the swamplands or flutter through the woods - storks pacing the pools in search of muddy catfish, or vultures climbing upwards and upwards on thermals of warm air towards the clouds. A sojourn in Katavi means joining a select group of insiders who have discovered one of Africa's best-kept secrets - a remnant of true wilderness, safe from the rigours of human 'progress'.

Chada Camp

A stay at Chada camp feels like being entertained on a private safari by old friends. The million acres of wilderness that surround the camp give a sense of being far removed from the everyday world, with its rules, regulations and petty annoyances. Information packs and personalised stationary are nowhere to be seen, and chocolates on pillows are most definitely out.

The food is similarly relaxed. Whatever Roland Purcell, the camp's owner, flies in from Arusha on his Cessna plane - patés, cheeses, a nice bottle of wine - is served under the shade of fig trees at lunchtime, accompanied perhaps by a slice of quiche or a salad dressed with olive oil. Picnics are prepared for consumption in a stand of palm trees, overlooking a stream teeming with wading birds and bulging with hippo.

In the evening, dinner is served round a single table in the mess tent, with conversation and bonhomie accompanying fresh fish, a roast leg of lamb, or a robust soup. All this satisfying fare is prepared by the camp chefs in a deceptively rough and ready kitchen - just a blackened wood-burning stove, topped with a few iron kettles, and a charcoal fire, complete with an ancient tin trunk in which cakes are baked by being buried in the hot coals. Kebabs are cooked on a wire grille over the fire, and the camp stores are locked securely at night to protect against the hyenas who like to raid the larder.

garlic, leeks and celery and fry in about 5 tablespoons olive oil until soft but not brown. Then add the pumpkin and fry gently for about 5 minutes until soft.

Now blend the mixture with the stock and milk. Bring to the boil and simmer gently for 20 minutes to reduce slightly. Salt and pepper to taste. Wash the inside of the pumpkin with boiling water to remove raw pumpkin traces and warm the vessel. Pour in the soup and top with a knob of butter and a large pinch of chopped parsley.

Roast Katavi goat dressed as lamb
Serves 6

The lush grass of the Katavi area not only supports thousands of buffalo and antelope that live in the National Park, but also ensures that the local goat population boasts a meat that is as tender and tasty than most lamb you will ever taste. Of course this recipe is just as good with a fine leg of lamb.

One leg of young goat / lamb

4 sprigs rosemary

3 cloves garlic

4 tbs honey

8 tbs fine Dijon mustard

3 tbs olive oil

Pumpkin soup
Serves 6

One medium pumpkin (1kg approx)

1 large onion (150g chopped)

3 medium leeks (100g chopped)

2 sticks celery with leaves (80g chopped)

2 cloves garlic, crushed

500ml vegetable stock

500ml milk

Olive oil for frying

Salt and pepper

Parsley for garnish

Cut the lid from the pumpkin if you wish to use it as a serving vessel (otherwise just chop up and remove skin and seeds) scoop out the seeds and discard. With a small paring knife, carefully remove all of the flesh from the pumpkin. Finely chop the flesh and wash in fresh water to remove unwanted residue. Finely chop the onions,

Trim any excess fat from the leg. Chop the garlic cloves and rosemary. Dunk the garlic and rosemary into the olive oil. Stab deep into the thick flesh of the meat several times and insert wedges of garlic and sprigs of rosemary. Mix the honey and mustard together and smear all over the surface of the leg, rubbing salt onto the end of the leg. Roast in a moderate to hot oven (gas 7) for 25 minutes per 500g. Check the meat by pushing a skewer or fine knife into the flesh and observing the juice. Serve with potatoes, sweet potatoes, parsnips, carrots, onions, whole garlic cloves (all roasted) with french beans and broccoli for contrast. A delicious gravy can be made from the meat juices thickened with flour, thinned out with stock, simmered for a few minutes and seasoned with salt and pepper.

Lettow-Vorbeck's lassi

This smooth lassi accompanies our tiffin picnics, brought in by Land Rover and set out under a shady tamarind tree. This recipe makes one litre.

500ml yoghurt
250ml milk
3 tbs castor sugar
1 tsp cumin seeds
10g fresh ginger
500g papaya flesh
200g peeled banana

Heat a dry frying pan and throw in the cumin seeds, tossing until they have turned dark brown. Then grind them in a pestle and mortar. Peel and grate the ginger and blend all of the ingredients together. Cool in a fridge for a couple of hours. Pour over crushed ice when ready to serve. Add a tot of rum per glass to make the delicious 'Lettow's Last Stand' cocktail.

Chada heart stopper (Créme Brulee)

1 Madagascar vanilla pod
2 level tbs castor sugar
4 level tbs demerara sugar
12 egg yolks
2.5 pints single cream

If your heart hasn't beaten fast enough watching the lion kill, we give it a major kick at dinner afterwards.If you can't get vanilla pods, forget the first paragraph of the recipe and just add three drops of vanilla essence to the mixture.

Put the cream in a bowl over a pan of very softly boiling water with the vanilla pod. Leave to infuse for half an hour.

Carefully stir in the egg yolks, beaten with caster sugar. Cook very slowly until the cream is thick enough to coat the back of a spoon. Strain the cream and chill for four hours or so into a large dish. Sprinkle the sifted Demerara sugar on top of the chilled cream and set in a larger ovenproof bowl filled with ice-cubes and put under the charcoal grill to brown until the sugar has caramelized. Chill again for a few hours.

Arusha

Early in the twentieth century Arusha town consisted of a few rickety store buildings selling everything from rifles to tinned vegetables. The town boasted one tiny hotel, known as Blooms, where hardy German settlers gathered to drink and carouse alongside a few British residents and passing hunters sipping gin and tonic in the bar. For all the glamour of its white hunters and safari clients - the Prince of Wales attended a party at the Arusha hotel in 1928 - Arusha remained a small hunting and farming community, surrounded by vast wheat and grain farming regions on the slopes of Kilimanjaro. Like Nairobi, Arusha retained a 'wild west' flavour until well into the 20th century, but unlike its Kenyan counterpart, the town was not predominantly British, but had a more international flavour.

Today, although Arusha's central position on the continent remains unchanged, most of the town, with its hardware shops, curio stalls and internet cafes, would be unrecognisable to the farmers and white hunters who lived there in the town's formative years. Away from the hustle and bustle of the town centre, however, still lie a few small highland settlements that seem to have changed very little since the early years of the twentieth century - pockets of tranquillity where mountain streams rush through forested valleys, steep paths rise up past banana and coconut plantations, and neat rows of coffee plants bisect green hillsides.

Ngare Sero
Mountain Lodge

The still, impossibly clear waters of the river that runs past the front of Ngare Sero Lodge provide a peaceful place to relax with a sundowner while watching the white egrets fly by in the evening. But the river has another, more practical function. Flowing downstream from the tranquil pools that front the old colonial farmhouse, the water is directed via a 1920s turbine system into hatcheries and breeding pools for dapper, iridescent rainbow trout.

The trout from Ngare Sero's fish farm are sold commercially all over Tanzania, but guests at Ngare Sero can enjoy them first - smoked, roasted, baked or steamed - straight from the river and onto the plate. Those guests who prefer to catch their own dinner are welcome to try their luck at still-water fly fishing in the hotel's well-stocked trout pool.

Naturally trout are not the sole item on the menu at Ngare Sero. Wineberries - a sweeter, more succulent cousin of the raspberry - are harvested wild from the forest by the local community and used to make tangy sorbets or crisp tarts. Bread and pizzas are baked in the open air ovens that adjoin the farmhouse, before being laid out on the massive oak sideboard for dinner or lunch in the formal, medieval-style dining rooms.

Trout quiche

Serves 5

Pastry:

350g plain flour

Pinch of salt

225g vegetable fat

A little cold water to mix

Filling:

2 eggs

50g grated cheese

250ml milk

100g smoked trout (cut small)

1 small onion

30g butter

Combine flour, fat salt in a basin with a little cold water and mix to make pastry. Line the dish and bake pastry case blind for about 10 minutes. Beat the eggs in a basin and add cheese, seasoning and milk. Melt the butter in small pan, add bacon and onions, cook slowly until just brown then turn into the egg mixture. Mix and pour into the pastry case and bake in the oven at 180 to 200C for about 5 minutes.

Trout with herbs and butter steamed in foil

Serves 1

1 trout of 500g or more

120g butter

120ml oil

1 clove garlic

Fresh parsley and dill

1 large lemon

50ml white wine

Clean trout leaving head and fins on, rub plenty of salt inside the cavity, rub exterior with butter, lay fish on cooking foil. Mix oil, wine, lemon juice and herbs and pour around the fish. Lay a square of aluminium cooking foil onto a baking dish. Place trout on foil and fold corners leaving air space inside. Place baking dish in a medium oven and cook for about 10 minutes per 500g of fish. Present at table on serving dish still in foil to preserve the aromas. Serve with cress and steamed vegetables.

Wineberry sorbet

Serves 6

1kg wineberries

250g sugar

Juice of half a lemon and half an orange

250ml water

125ml yoghurt (optional)

Liquidise the berries then sieve to remove pips, add lemon and orange juice. Boil sugar and water for 5 minutes, cool and add to berries. Place in container and freeze. To serve scrape out in slivers. Yoghurt may be added to the mix to give a light ice cream effect.

Chicken Ballantine

Serves 4

4 chicken breasts

2 eggs

50g breadcrumbs

65g butter

1 bunch parsley

6 cloves garlic

Blend butter with finely chopped parsley and garlic, wrap and chill. Take breasts of chicken, remove skin and lightly beat flat. Separate the inner fillet and lay thick slice of parsley butter on breast, cover with fillet and roll tightly, paste with beaten egg and fix with a skewer. Cover with beaten egg and roll in breadcrumbs. Chill again. Fry in covered pan turning occasionally. Serve with sauté potatoes.

Oldonyo Orok

Ol Donyo Orok, meaning 'Black Mountain' in Maasai, is a low-key yet very stylish lodge set in the shadow of the awesome, towering crater of Mount Meru, just outside Arusha National Park. It was here that scenes from the 1962 Hollywood movie 'Hatari', starring John Wayne, were shot. The film, the rollicking tale of a group of professional animal catchers in the African bush, also starred Hardy Kruger, a tall, blonde German film star making his break into Hollywood by playing Wayne's handsome driver, Chris Mercer. The tall tale had an interesting real-life ending - Kruger liked the farmhouse that had been built for the film set so much he bought the property for himself after the movie was in the can. He later added another ranch house style building, and used the property as a combined farm and hunting lodge for many years afterwards.

The lodge building is a simple, whitewashed mud-brick structure, but the interior is stunningly decorated with low stone benches, a massive open fireplace and a wooden mezzanine floor.

Food here has an Italian feel, with hearty pastas, focaccia bread and grilled meats served either around the elegant wooden dining table, or outside against the dramatic backdrop of Mount Meru. At night, the fire blazes merrily, and candles light the sitting room for evenings spent lolling on soft cream cushions and sipping red wine.

Avocado soup

Serves 1-2

1 small onion
1 well ripened avocado
1 chicken cube
1 pint warm water
Single cream to taste
Juice of 1/2 a lime
Salt and pepper

Finely chop the small onion. Mouli the avocado. Melt the chicken cube in the warm water and slowly add the stock to the onion and avocado, until the consistency is that of a thick soup. Then add a few spoonfuls of single cream. Season with salt, pepper and a squeeze of lime. Garnish with finely chopped chives and serve with focaccia.

Focaccia bread

Serves 1-2

350g plain flour
Pinch salt
2 tsp yeast
3 tbs olive oil
250ml warm water
Rosemary, salt, black pepper for topping

Sift the flour and salt into a large bowl. In a separate bowl, mix yeast into the water and leave until frothy. Mix olive oil into the flour then gradually add the water until the flour turns to a dough which leaves the sides of the bowl clean. Lightly flour a surface and turn the dough out onto it and knead until bouncy and elastic. Return it to the bowl and cover with clingfilm or a damp tea towel and leave in a warm place until it has doubled in size. Roll out bread dough to about half a centimetre or less, then leave to rise to about 1 centimetre. Stab surface with fork, drizzle generously with olive oil, sprinkle generously with salt, add some black pepper & crush on fresh rosemary. Bake in charcoal oven until golden.

Real Italian pasta sauce

Serves 1-2

1 large onion, coarsely chopped
2 or 3 cloves garlic
1 tin or 500g Italian plum tomatoes, chopped
Extra virgin olive oil
Salt and black pepper

Fry onion and garlic in olive oil - do not brown. Add tomatoes. Simmer for approximately 20 minutes, or until the tomato juice has reduced and the sauce is thick and dark red. Season with salt & black pepper. Garnish with fresh basil, & serve with freshly grated parmesan.

Special charcoal grilled chicken

Serves 4

4 pieces of chicken
For the marinade:
250ml olive oil
Juice of 1 lime
1 tsp cumin seeds
1 tbs freshly chopped chives
2 tsp chopped garlic,
1 tsp chillis
Salt and pepper
Pinch freshly chopped flat leaf parsley

Cut chicken into 4 pieces. Mix all marinade ingredients together and marinate chicken for at least 2 hours, turning every half hour. Grill over charcoal, basting regularly with the marinade using a bunch of rosemary. Do not make coals too hot OR too cool, either one will dry out your chicken. Serve with rosemary potatoes & a fresh rocket salad.

.

Safari Spa

The emphasis at the beautiful farmhouse of Safari Spa is on healthy living - hard and fast polo matches in the shadow of Kilimanjaro, a relaxing wallow in the marble jacuzzi of the spa, or an afternoon's workout in the fully equipped gym that's housed in one of the beautifully converted farm outbuildings.

As one would expect therefore, the food served in between such activities is wholesome and nutritious, comprising mostly plain farmhouse cooking in keeping with Safari Spa's original function as a coffee plantation, and its current role as the centre of a thriving rose farm.

Light lunches of goulash soup and salad are served in the pavilion that overlooks the swimming pool, set among palms and bouganvilleas in the impeccably landscaped gardens. Fresh farm raspberries and yoghurt appear for breakfast, taken on the balcony of the mess building, framed by jacaranda trees against the blue highland sky.

Dinner is a grander affair, taken 'Out of Africa' style from crisp white table linen and served by waiters in flowing white robes in a dining room decorated with antique brass lamps and oil paintings. Upstairs in the lounge, a corner fireplace provides a cosy focal point for an after-dinner drink on the leopard-print sofa.

Safari Spa special smoothie

Serves 1

1 large banana

1 orange

1 lemon/lime,

1 tsp honey

5 cubes of ice.

Cut and squeeze all the above ingredients and blend well. This makes a large glass of very tasty, healthy smoothie. Decorate the glass with one slice of orange.

Hungarian goulash soup

Serves 2

1 medium size beef fillet

2 big onions

1 tbs butter

2 tbs sweet red Hungarian or Spanish paprika powder

2 fresh tomatoes

6 medium potatoes

1 green pepper

6 cloves garlic,

Salt and pepper to taste.

Cut the onions into small cubes and put in a big pot with the butter. Fry on a gentle heat until the onions get soft then remove the heat and sprinkle over the paprika powder. Return to heat for one minute, stirring continuously (this is important to avoid burning the paprika powder - this method gives a very special taste to the food). After that, add the small cubes of cut fillet, tomato, green pepper, garlic, salt, pepper. Stir and put back on the heat for about 20 minutes. Add the potatoes and about one and half a litres of water. Let it stew for a good hour. Garnish with some parsley and serve with fresh garlic bread.

Garlic bread

Serves 2-3

200g butter

20 crushed garlic cloves

Fresh parsley

Salt and pepper

1 loaf French bread

Big piece of foil

Slice the bread partially through, spread the garlic butter both sides of the slices, and wrap it in the foil. Bake in a hot oven for half an hour.

Beef Curry

Serves 2

1 medium size beef fillet

1 tbs butter

2 medium size onions

5 cloves garlic

1 tsp ginger paste

1 tbs curry powder

2 big fresh tomatoes

1 tbs tomato paste

Salt and pepper

Touch of chilli

1 glass red wine

1 tbs natural yoghurt

Cut the beef, onions, garlic and fresh tomato into small cubes. Fry the onions in the butter, then add the beef cubes, salt, pepper, curry powder, chilli and tomatoes. Stir and fry for about 20 minutes. Then add the glass of red wine and 2 glasses of warm water. Stir and stew it on a slow heat for about an hour. Add 3 tbs of natural yoghurt and cook for another 5 minutes. Garnish with parsley. Serve with brown or white rice and traditional chapatis.

**The authors would like to extend heartfelt thanks to the following people
for invaluable assistance during the course of the Safari Living Recipes project:**

Hon Zakia Meghji, Minister for Tourism and Natural Resources, Director General Mr Bigurube and Public Relations Manager Mr James Lembeli of TANAPA, Mr Emmanuel Chausi of Ngorongoro Crater Conservation Area, Benson Kibonde of Selous Game Reserve, Caroline Blummer at Regional Air, Rashida Patwa and Anna Westh at Coastal Aviation, Gulf Air in London, David Sem at Precision Air, Shayne Richardson and Martine Karpes of CC Africa, Roland and Zoe Purcell of Greystoke Safaris, Dean Yeardon of Halcyon Ltd, Chris Fox of Mwagusi Safari Camp, Charles Dobie of Selous Safari Company, Marlise Alpers of Sanctuary Lodges, Salim Janmohamed and Shafina Mohamed of Serena Hotels, Pratik and Sonia Patel of Tanzania Photographic Safaris, Nuru and Khairoon Jafferji in Dar es Salaam, Zulfiqar Khanbhai, Abdul and Salma Khanbhai, Hatim and Rashida Khanbhai and Justin and Gillian Bell in Arusha.

At the camps, the authors are indebted to the following people for making each photoshoot possible:

Rawanna and Murray at Chada Camp, Tonya and Pete at Crater Lodge, Dale and Margaret at Gibb's Farm, Jimmy and Daniela at Greystoke Camp, Peter at Grumeti River Lodge, Neil at Jongomero, Faustini at Kleins Camp, Hilda at Kikoti Camp, Charles and Hannah at Kirawira, Colin and Karen at Kusini Camp, Francis and Naringo at Maji Moto, Patrick at Migration Camp, Helle at Mwagusi Camp, Simon at Naitolia, Mike, Tim, Stasia and Gisella at Ngare Sero Mountain Lodge, Corbett and Camilla at Ol Donyo Orok, Paul and Tati at Oliver's Camp, Peter and Sarah at Ruaha River Lodge, Zsusza and Jerome at Safari Spa, Julieta at Sand Rivers Selous, Sal, Vonan and Nicky at Selous Safari Camp, Francis at Lake Manyara Serena, Damian, Johnny and team at Sokwe, Glen and Cindy at Swala Camp, Alfred at Tarangire Treetops, and Annette and John of Tarangire Safari Lodge.

Thanks also to Mervin Ng in Singapore, to Sean Qureshi of Spectrum Colour Lab in Nairobi, Zarina Jafferji for her help on our Tarangire photoshoot, to Shabani our tireless driver, to Terence, Antony and Ali here at Zanzibar Gallery Publishers, Bobby McKenna for proof editing and to Abid and Bashira Jafferji for all their help and support. Finally, many thanks to my dearest wife Kulsum for her patience during my long absences on safari.

Page 85: Text by Geoffrey Weill, CCAfrica

Contact Addresses

Chada Camp
Greystoke Safaris
PO Box 681, Usa River, Tanzania
Tel: +255 27 255 3820/3821
Email: info@mahale.co.tz
www.mahale.co.tz

Gibbs Farm
PO Box 6084, Arusha, Tanzania
Tel: +255 27 250 6702
Fax: +255 27 250 8310
Email: gibbs@habari.co.tz
www.gibbsfarm.net

Greystoke Camp
PO Box 681, Usa River, Tanzania
Tel: +255 27 255 3820/3821
Email: info@mahale.co.tz
www.mahale.co.tz

Grumeti River Camp
Conservation Corporation Africa
P/Bag X27, Benmore, 2010,
Johannesburg
Block F, Pinmill Farm, Katherine St,
Sandton, South Africa
Tel: +27 11 809 4300
Fax: +27 11 809 4400
Email: webenquiries@ccafrica.com
www.ccafrica.com

Kikoti Camp
PO Box 284, Arusha, Tanzania
Tel: +255 27 2508790
Fax: +255 27 2508896
Email: tzphotosafaris@habari.co.tz
www.tzphotosafaris.com

Kirawira Luxury Tented Camp
Serena Hotels Ltd
6th Floor, AICC, Ngorongoro Wing
PO Box 2551, Arusha, Tanzania
Tel: +255 27 2506304
Fax: +255 27 2504155
Email: reservations@serena.co.tz
www.serenahotels.com

Klein's Camp
Conservation Corporation Africa
P/Bag X27, Benmore, 2010,
Johannesburg
Block F, Pinmill Farm, Katherine St,
Sandton, South Africa
Tel: +27 11 809 4300

Fax: +27 11 809 4400
Email: webenquiries@ccafrica.com
www.ccafrica.com

Kusini Camp
Sanctuary Lodges
Tel: +255 27 250 98 16
Fax +255 27 250 8273
Email:
tanzania@sanctuarylodges.com
www.sanctuarylodges.com

Lake Manyara Tree Lodge
Conservation Corporation Africa
P/Bag X27, Benmore, 2010,
Johannesburg
Block F, Pinmill Farm, Katherine St,
Sandton, South Africa
Tel: +27 11 809 4300
Fax: +27 11 809 4400
Email: webenquiries@ccafrica.com
www.ccafrica.com

Lake Manyara Serena
Serena Hotels Ltd
6th Floor, AICC, Ngorongoro Wing
PO Box 2551, Arusha, Tanzania
Tel: +255 27 2506304
Fax: +255 27 2504155
Email: reservations@serena.co.tz
www.serenahotels.com

Migration Camp
Halcyon Tanzania Ltd
PO Box 1861, Arusha
Tel/Fax: +255 27 250 9277 ñ 81
Email: res@halcyontz.com
www.halcyontz.com

Mwagusi Camp
Tropic Africa
14 Castelnau
London SW13 9RU
Tel/fax: +44 208 846 9363
Email: tropicafrica.uk@virgin.net
www.ruaha.org

Naitolia
The Adventure Centre
PO Box 1215, Arusha, Tanzania
Tel: +255 744 371345
Email:
naitolia@tarangireconservation.com

Ngare Sero Mountain Lodge
PO Box 425, Arusha
Tel: +255 27 255 3638
Email:
ngare-sero-lodge@habari.co.tz

Ngorongoro Crater Lodge
Conservation Corporation Africa
P/Bag X27, Benmore, 2010,
Johannesburg
Block F, Pinmill Farm,
Katherine St, Sandton, South Africa
Tel: +27 11 809 4300
+27 11 809 4400
Email: webenquiries@ccafrica.com
www.ccafrica.com

Ol Donyo Orok
PO Box 104, Usa River, Tanzania
Tel: +255 27 2553868
Email:bishop@yako.habari.co.tz

Oliver's Camp
PO Box 425, Arusha, Tanzania
Tel/fax: +255 27 2508548
Email: olivers@habari.co.tz
www.oliverscamp.com

Ruaha River Lodge
Foxtreks Ltd
PO Box 10270, Dar es Salaam, TZ
Tel: +255 741 237422
Fax: +255 741 327706
Email: fox@twiga.com
www.ruahariverlodge.com

Safari Spa
PO Box 988, Arusha, Tanzania
Tel: +255 27 2553264
Email: safarispa@habari.co.tz

Sand Rivers Selous
PO Box 1344, Dar es Salaam, TZ
Tel: +255 741 768153
Fax: +255 22 2865156
Email: sand-rivers@intafrica.com
www.sandrivers.com

Selous Safari Camp
PO Box 1192, Dar es Salaam, TZ
Tel: +255 22 2134794
Fax: +255 22 2112794
Email:info@selous.com
www.selous.com

Sokwe
PO Box 3052, Arusha, Tanzania
Tel: +255 27 2548182
Fax: +255 27 2548320
Email: enquiries@sokwe.com
www.sokwe.com

Swala Camp
Sanctuary Lodges
Tel +255 27 250 98 16
Email:
tanzania@sanctuarylodges.com
www.sanctuarylodges.com

Tarangire Safari Lodge
PO Box 2703, Arusha, Tanzania
Tel: +255 27 2531447
Email: sss@habari.co.tz

Tarangire Treetops
Halcyon Tanzania Ltd
PO Box 1861, Arusha
Tel/Fax: +255 27 250 9277 ñ 81
Email: res@halcyontz.com

**The following airlines provide
internal flights within Tanzania:**

Coastal Aviation
PO Box 3052, Dar es Salaam TZ
Tel: +255 22 2117959
Fax: +255 22 2118647
Email: safari@coastal.cc
www.coastal.cc

Precision Air
PO Box 1636, Arusha, Tanzania
Tel: +255 27 2506903
Fax: +255 27 2508204
Email:
information@precisionairtz.com
www.precisionairtz.com

Regional Air
PO Box 14755, Arusha, Tanzania
Tel: +255 27 2502541
Fax: +255 27 2544164
Email: info@regional.co.tz
www.airkenya.com

The Photographer

Javed Jafferji studied photography, film and television in the UK, before returning to Tanzania to publish various books, including Historical Zanzibar - Romance of the Ages; Images of Zanzibar; Zanzibar Stone Town - an Architectural Exploration; Zanzibar - an Essential Guide, Tanzania - African Eden, A Taste of Zanzibar, Zanzibar Style, Safari Living, and Zanzibar Style Recipes.

His work has been published in national and international newspapers and magazines including The Times, Newsweek and Geo. He has held exhibitions in London, Paris, Berlin and Pakistan as well as Tanzania.

Javed also publishes a magazine called 'The Swahili Coast' to promote eco-tourism in Zanzibar and Pemba, manages a photography and design studio and runs a gift shop, the Zanzibar Gallery, which sells gifts, clothes, books and antiques.

The Stylist

Kulsum Jafferji, Javed's wife, runs the Zanzibar Gallery, a bookshop and craft gallery in the heart of Zanzibar's Stone Town. Her interest in food styling developed over the course of many photographic trips with Javed to Tanzania's best hotels, lodges and safari camps.

The Writer

Gemma Pitcher fell in love with Africa when she was seventeen and has been returning as often as possible ever since. She studied English Literature at Exeter University, UK, and worked as a safari consultant and editor before starting a career as a freelance travel writer. She has contributed to the *Bradt Guide to Zanzibar* and written articles for several international magazines as well as authoring the title *Zanzibar Style*.

Zanzibar Style, also by Javed Jafferji and Gemma Pitcher, was voted one of the 'Top 20 Travel Books for Christmas 2001' by the UK's Times newspaper.